# Dancing with Angels in Heaven

*Tidings of Hope from the Spirit Realm*

by

Garnet Schulhauser

For permission, serialization, condensation, adaptions, or for our catalog of other publications, write to Ozark Mountain Publishing, Inc., P.O. Box 754, Huntsville, AR 72740, ATTN: Permissions Department.

Library of Congress Cataloging-in-Publication Data

Garnet Schulhauser -1951-

*Dancing with Angels in Heaven* by Garnet Schulhauser

In his fifth book, the author recalls a trip to the Spirit Side to observe an orientation class about planet Earth for souls planning to incarnate on our planet.

1. Spiritual 2. Astral Travel 3. Spirit Guides 4. Afterlife
I. Garnet Schulhauser, 1951 II. Metaphysical III. Afterlife IV. Title

Library of Congress Catalog Card Number: 2021933122
ISBN: 9781950608034

Cover Art and Layout: Victoria Cooper Art
Book set in: Times New Roman and Battlefin
Book Design: Summer Garr
Published by:

OZARK
MOUNTAIN
PUBLISHING

PO Box 754, Huntsville, AR 72740
800-935-0045 or 479-738-2348; fax 479-738-2448
WWW.OZARKMT.COM

Printed in the United States of America

# ⚜ *Acknowledgments* ⚜

I am eternally grateful to Albert for appearing in my life the way he did, and for all his guidance and wisdom, as I navigated my way through a new and exciting chapter of my life. It has not all been a bed of roses, but his steady hand has guided me through all the rough patches on the road to spiritual enlightenment. His revelations have provided me with a clear understanding of life, death, the afterlife, and the cycle of reincarnation on Earth. And I sincerely hope his truths have made a positive impact on everyone who has read my books.

Of course, I would not have been able to enroll as Albert's messenger without the unwavering support from my family: my wife, Cathy, sons Blake and Colin, daughters-in-law Lauren and Bergis, and grandchildren Kymera, Darian, and Ronan. I am blessed with a loving family that somehow manages to ignore all my human foibles.

And all of my efforts to deliver spiritual enlightenment to humankind would likely have gone for naught but for the encouragement I have received from all the people who read my books, listened to my radio show interviews, or heard my conference presentations. For these people, my gratitude has no bounds.

Special thanks goes to Dolores Cannon, who is now working her magic from the Spirit Side, for agreeing to publish my first book. Her tradition of excellence has been continued by her daughters, Julia and Nancy, with the able assistance of all the staff at Ozark Mountain Publishing.

# ᕦᕤ Contents ᕦᕤ

# ༄ Introduction ༄

Wonders never cease! Prior to meeting my spirit guide, Albert, disguised as a homeless man, back in May of 2007, I was a condescending, stuffed-shirt corporate lawyer who was self-absorbed in pursuit of the good life I believed could be attained with diligence and hard work. In those days, I had neither religion nor spirituality as a moral compass, and I had to rely on my upbringing to provide me with me with the guidelines I needed to operate in a society that seemed to be hell-bent on accumulating money and power.

After meeting Albert on the street that fateful day, the vacuum left in my life after tossing religion into the trash can began to fill with the ineffable joy of spiritual enlightenment, and my life has never been the same. My dialogue and astral travels with Albert have opened my eyes to the vastness and diversity of life in the universe, and I now appreciate the intricacy of the cycle of reincarnation on our planet. Spirituality has filled the void left by religion, and I now understand who I am and how I am connected to the Source and to everyone else.

Once I made the decision to come out of the spiritual closet by publishing my first book, things were never the same, but I have no regrets about leaving the practice of law and becoming an author of spiritual books. I lost a few friends along the way (some of whom likely think I am suffering from an early onset of dementia); however, I gained many new friends who have encouraged me to continue writing about the revelations from Albert and the other wise souls I met during my travels.

Since publishing my first book in 2012, I have been actively disseminating Albert's messages through book-signing tours, conference presentations, YouTube interviews, and as a guest on over one hundred and sixty radio talk shows. I am encouraged by the warm reception I have received, as it clearly indicates an ever-increasing number of people are expanding their consciousness and becoming spiritually aware. I am optimistic this trend will continue to grow as more and more people cast aside the dark side of humanity as they follow the path toward spiritual enlightenment.

This book is a sequel to my first four books, *Dancing on a Stamp*, *Dancing Forever with Spirit*, *Dance of Heavenly Bliss*, and *Dance of Eternal Rapture*, as it recounts my most recent encounters with Albert. As with the first four books, Albert had a carefully planned agenda designed to teach me (and all humankind) a lesson or to provide us with a few nuggets of wisdom to help us understand who we are in the grand scheme of things and why we left the bliss of the Spirit Side to have a human journey on Earth.

My astral trips with Albert revealed the vast diversity of life in the universe (including intelligent life forms on other planets), and I now realize how little I know about the infinite cosmos spawned long ago by the Source. Every new morsel of information I distilled from my dialogue with Albert, and the astral trips that followed, are like pieces of a gigantic jigsaw puzzle that one day will reveal the entire picture about the Source and the cycle of reincarnation on Earth.

Albert has been a guiding light to follow—a beacon of wisdom and love who has encouraged me to break out of my comfort zone and disseminate his revelations to humanity. Albert and I have shared many lives together on this planet, and I know he has been a loyal friend throughout. Although he is dedicated to spreading the message of love and hope from Spirit, at times he can be cheeky, flippant, and a bit of a rascal. This is his way of telling us we should not take life so seriously because no matter what we do during our lives we will always return to the Spirit Realm when we have finished our human journeys.

What happens on Earth stays on Earth, except for the

memories we retain from our experiences and the lessons we learned during our incarnations on this planet. We should view our lives on Earth as stimulating escapades designed to help us evolve as souls. Every soul is on an incomparable journey we chose for ourselves to gather knowledge and wisdom, comforted by the realization there is no "right" or "wrong" path to follow. All roads lead onward and upward, and we can never become lost or abandoned.

After finishing the manuscript for my fourth book, *Dance of Eternal Rapture*, I had been waiting for Albert to give me my marching orders on writing book five. He initially told me to put it on hold, so I could take the Quantum Healing Hypnosis Technique (QHHT) course and become a QHHT practitioner.

QHHT is an advanced hypnotherapy technique developed by Dolores Cannon, who is the founder of Ozark Mountain Publishing, Inc. It uses past life regression and contact with the Higher Self to reveal the answers sought by clients.

I followed Albert's advice and became a QHHT practitioner, something I found to be fascinating, enlightening, and gratifying.

The most important aspect of a QHHT session is the connection to the client's Higher Self, when the practitioner will converse with the Higher Self to find the answers to the questions brought to the session by the client. The Higher Self (also known as the Higher Consciousness, the Oversoul, the Universal Mind, or the Subconscious) is the all-knowing, higher part of our souls that dwells in the Spirit Realm and is always closely connected to the Source (God). The Higher Self has described themselves as a collective that exists at a higher level than our spirit guides.

The Higher Self has limitless knowledge and can answer any question the client poses, and it has an absolute and unrestricted ability to heal the physical body if it believes such healing would be appropriate for the client. The Higher Self knows people better than they know themselves, because it has been with them every step of the way in this life and all the other lives they have ever lived, and it remembers every little detail. The Higher Self also knows what souls had included in their Life Plans before they incarnated, so it is aware of the path they had hoped to follow and the challenges and lessons they wanted to encounter.

The Higher Self can answer questions about anything the client poses to it, including life purpose and career path, relationship issues with family or friends, tips on finding a suitable life partner, the genesis of health issues and how to alleviate or get rid of phobias and afflictions, finding financial abundance, the reason for inexplicable events (such as paranormal or ET encounters) or recurring dreams, the role of people from past lives in a client's current life and whether there is any negative karma with them that must be resolved, the identity of a person's spirit guides and how best to communicate with them, as well as information about ET abductions and implants, the New Earth, life on other planets, and anything else the client is curious about.

For these reasons, the wisdom clients can obtain from the Higher Self will provide divine enlightenment to help them enjoy a much more meaningful life. The role of a QHHT practitioner is to facilitate a direct connection to a client's Higher Self to tap into its limitless knowledge and transform the person's life for the better. (For more information on QHHT, please go to my website: www. garnetschulhauserqhht.com.)

I get a lot of satisfaction from helping clients achieve a greater understanding of who they are and what they should be doing to fulfill their destiny, and the many positive comments I get from satisfied clients is really icing on the cake. I have received numerous testimonials from happy clients, and I would like to share with you one I got recently from a very bright and talented young lady:

"My QHHT session with Garnet was truly life changing! He does a phenomenal job at clearly explaining everything about the process and has a very calm energy, which makes the conversations very comfortable. Upon listening to my session recording, I was incredibly impressed with how he intuitively guided the questions, extracting as much information as possible, both from the past life and my Higher Self. He did such a thorough job, eliciting useful details and answers to questions I didn't even know that I had in the first place! He is such a warm, kind and wise soul. I am eternally grateful for the opportunity he brought to me by facilitating this session. It was beyond enlightening and transformational ... and as a bonus, I was able to heal a skin condition that I had been living with for over eight years. Words cannot truly convey my deep appreciation and gratitude. Thank you Garnet."

Receiving testimonials like this is why conducting QHHT sessions is so rewarding for me. I now understand why Albert recommended the course to me, as it has opened new horizons on my spiritual journey. And then, when I was least expecting it, Albert tapped me on the shoulder and told me to sharpen my pencil, as the time had come to begin writing the manuscript for my fifth book.

I urge everyone to consider Albert's truths carefully and embrace them fully if they ring true in your heart. If you prefer to stick with your own beliefs, however, there is no downside, and you should continue to follow your instincts. Albert has mentioned many times it does not matter what people believe during their human incarnation, because at the end of the day we will all end up in the same place, and the truth will be known to all.


—Garnet Schulhauser

# ᨓᨓ Chapter One ᨓᨓ
## *Orientation to Planet Earth*

I was roused from my deep slumber by a noise I could not place. I sat up in bed and looked around, but I could see nothing unusual as the silvery moonlight streamed in through the windows. And then a wispy apparition appeared in the doorway and moved toward my bed.

I relaxed as I could now see my dear friend and guide, Albert, had returned. His astral form floated effortlessly in the moonlight, as he offered me one of his warm smiles. I was thrilled to have him back in my life, and I was eager to see what he had in mind for me this time.

"Hello, Albert," I greeted him. "What brings you here today?"

"I have a few surprises for you. Are you up for another adventure?"

"Sign me up, Albert. I need a little more excitement in my life, something to get the juices flowing again."

"I will have to be careful in that regard, because I do not want to impair your health," Albert retorted. "At your age, you can become overly excited if you find two prizes in the Cracker Jack box, instead of the usual one. And the other day your heartbeat went through the roof when you found a dime on the street."

I gave Albert a painful wince and fired back: "Pardon me while I roll on the floor laughing. You humor is really cutting edge—have you been attending comedy school in your spare time?"

And then, as he had done many times before, Albert reached out to grab my astral hand and then tugged until he had pulled my astral body out of my physical body. Without further ado, he guided me up through the ceiling and the wispy clouds hanging in the night sky until we came to a stop high above our beautiful planet. Once again, I got to marvel at the breathtaking splendor of the blue orb floating in the darkness of the void, a scene that seemed more spectacular with every visit.

With a gentle nudge, Albert led me through the shimmering doorway to the Spirit Side. The meadow on the other side seemed even more inviting than before, as we strolled through the lush green grass and past the profusion of fragrant wildflowers proudly displaying their vibrant blooms in a myriad of colors.

Beside the gleaming white city of Aglaia, we paused under a giant redwood tree and settled down on a wooden bench nestled beside the roses bordering the stone path.

The soft light that seemed to emanate from everywhere wrapped the meadow with a warm embrace, as the songbirds chirped a heavenly opus to the gods.

We were soon joined by a familiar figure from my previous travels with Albert. Sophia, the Chair of the Council of Wise Ones, projected an aura of love, compassion, and wisdom that never failed to astound. She greeted us with a warm smile that lit up her regal face with an inner glow.

I recalled my first meeting with Sophia on my initial trip to the Spirit Side. In the white city of Aglaia Albert had guided me toward a stately building at the far end of the plaza, a magnificent structure with Grecian pillars lining the front. When we reached the front of the building, which he called the Hall of Wisdom, we entered through the wide-open doorway. At the end of a long hallway we stopped in front of a grand door made of burnished brass, and Albert announced our presence with the round doorknocker. Upon hearing the word "enter" from inside, Albert opened the door and we stepped into the room.

It was large and circular, with a high domed ceiling. The room was well lit without any visible light fixtures, as the light seemed to emanate from the walls. In the center of the room was a table in the form of a semicircle, with the open section facing the door. The table was black and smooth, like gleaming granite, and it seemed to float in place without legs or any other visible means of support.

There were eleven people seated at this table, facing the center of the semicircle where Albert and I stood. They wore long gold-colored robes with a white sash tied around the waist. They looked very regal, with snow-white hair and smooth unwrinkled skin. Seated at the center was a striking woman with intense blue eyes, who Albert said was Sophia, the Chair of the panel.

Sophia revealed that Albert had brought me to the Spirit Side, the place I came from before I incarnated on Earth. It has a much higher vibration frequency than Earth, and it cannot normally be seen by people on Earth. It exists beyond the veil and is known to some people as Home, the Other Side, or Heaven. She advised I would return here once again when my life on Earth was finished, but my visit that time would be short because I still had many things to accomplish before I could leave my current incarnation.

She explained that I was standing in front of the Council of Wise Ones, whose job it was to oversee all the incarnations on Earth. The Council provides guidance and counseling to all souls before they begin their lives on Earth, and they assist returning souls with the analysis of the lives they have completed. Their main function is to help souls design Life Plans that will enable them to grow and evolve through their experiences on Earth.

The Council strives to ensure the lives that are chosen by souls are not too difficult for them (which can hinder their evolution if they rebel too much against the harshness of the life) or too easy, without appropriate lessons to be learned and challenges to overcome. They also counsel souls currently incarnated on Earth—to assist them with any adjustments to their Life Plans that may be desirable. Like all other souls, she pointed out that I travel to the Spirit Side every night during sleep to consult with the Council and my guides, but I don't remember these trips because I pass through the shroud of forgetfulness every morning when I return to my physical body.

I snapped out of my reverie when Sophia stood up and said: "Albert and I are about to teach an orientation class for souls who have never incarnated on Earth but are planning to do so. You can tag along with us if you want to watch the proceedings."

Without hesitation I followed Sophia and Albert into the white city and down a side street to the edge of the amphitheater built into the side of a hill. The seats were filled with souls of every description: globes of light, humans in long robes, and even a few alien humanoids. I was not surprised because Albert had told me souls on the Spirit Side can appear to others in any form they desire, but in their natural state they appear as globes of light. I assumed the souls appearing as humans were trying to get used to the human form, while the alien humanoids were displaying the physical characteristics they had last used when incarnating on the denser planes.

Sophia and Albert marched down the stairs and took center stage, while I sat down in the front row. As soon as the chatter subsided, Sophia began her address to the crowd.

"Welcome to your orientation to planet Earth. My name is Sophia, and I am the Chair of the Council of Wise Ones. And this is my co-lecturer, Albert, who has enjoyed many lives on Earth and has much wisdom to share about incarnating on Earth.

"You are all here today because you have never before incarnated on Earth, but you have expressed a desire to do so. Albert and I will give you a quick orientation to the planet and the things to watch for when planning a life on Earth.

"All of you have had previous incarnations on various planets in our galaxy, so you understand the basics of incarnating into physical bodies on the denser planes. You have no doubt heard the Earth school is one of the toughest schools in the universe, and we commend you for having the courage to test your mettle in a life filled with significant challenges. Albert and I will help you understand the nuances of the cycle of reincarnation on Earth and give you guidance on how best to survive the trials and tribulations you will likely encounter on your journey.

"Our first piece of advice is to run like Hell, before it is too late. You have to be out of your mind to even consider a life on Earth, which already has too many crazy people wreaking havoc on the civilization."

There was an audible gasp from the audience, and Sophia laughed with delight as she reassured them she was only joking. She took on a more somber tone as she continued:

"To begin, we want you to understand the transition that is now happening on Earth and its implications for humans."

With a wave of her hand, a large holographic sphere, filled with swirling blue-and-white vapors, dropped down from the ceiling and hovered above the floor. The swirling vapors quickly dissipated, leaving behind a crystal-clear image of Earth, as seen from space. I could see the outlines of North and South America and Western Europe, which was partially covered with white clouds. It was breathtaking to see Earth from this viewpoint.

Sophia continued: "Earth and its human inhabitants are at a major inflection point in their history. Humans are in the process of expanding their consciousness and transitioning to a higher vibration frequency, but they still need a lot help to achieve this. If this does not occur in a timely fashion, the consequences could be tragic for Earth and all its inhabitants.

"This shift will allow those who have increased their vibratory rates to transition to Earth in a higher dimension—a place often referred to as the New Earth—where the negative aspects of life on Old Earth don't exist. The New Earth is a place where all its creatures, including humans, live in peace and harmony, without conflicts, wars, or crime—a planet filled with love, compassion, and forgiveness. In the New Earth humans do not pollute the atmosphere, the water, or the soil, and they do not abuse the other creatures on the planet. And all the negative emotions that have been prevalent throughout human history on the Old Earth, like fear, anger, hate, jealousy, and greed, are nonexistent.

"Some humans have already made the transition and many others are in the process of making the shift. Unfortunately, there are millions of humans who are not even aware of what is going on around them.

"Human civilization is at a very advanced stage right now. They have created advanced technology that has made life much easier for most people; however, this technology has not been universally beneficial for everyone. Many people on Earth do not have enough food to eat or clean water to drink, and not everyone lives in a comfortable house, has access to the internet, or is free from the fear of arbitrary violence. Furthermore, humans' advanced technology, with its weapons of mass destruction, can destroy all living creatures on the planet if it is used in an irresponsible way.

"Earth has been home to many advanced civilizations in the past, like Lemuria and Atlantis, and none of them has survived. Several were destroyed by the actions of some of their citizens, driven by greed and the lust for power, who used technology to pursue their own goals. And whenever these civilizations collapsed, humanity had to start all over again. Humans are now once again at a similar stage of development, and they are facing the same crucial test: can they avoid destroying their civilization so all humans will have the opportunity to transition up the vibratory ladder, or will they crash and burn like these other civilizations that flopped in the past?

"Mother Earth herself is becoming impatient with humans and their abusive behavior. She is weary of humans who abuse other creatures and pollute her oceans and rivers, her fertile soil, and her atmosphere, with toxic chemicals, noxious emissions, and tons and tons of unsightly garbage. And make no mistake that Mother Earth can fight back—she can increase the number and intensity of natural disasters, such as earthquakes, floods, hurricanes, tornadoes, and volcanic eruptions, as a way of hitting back at humans. Ultimately, as a last resort, she has the ability to wipe out human civilization so she can start over again with a clean slate.

"For humans to avoid destroying their civilization with their own technology, or being wiped out by natural disasters, they must hasten the transition to the New Earth by increasing their vibratory rates and making the ascension to a new level of consciousness. To do so, they must learn to control their negative emotions and embrace love, compassion, and forgiveness.

"This is why humans must be especially vigilant during these times. Those people who are enlightened must be diligent with their efforts to help all humans make the shift, so human civilization will continue to flourish in the New Earth.

"The Council has been helping humans on Earth in many ways. We have been increasing the pace of the messages we are sending to humans about the coming transition, because time is becoming crucial. Our messages are sent through a host of different channels and messengers, with the hope more and more people will understand the problem and become part of the solution. Increasingly, we have enlisted more advanced souls to incarnate on the planet to assist humans through their leadership and wisdom. And many advanced civilizations on other planets in the universe have answered our call for help, and their assistance has been welcomed with open arms.

"We wanted to lay the groundwork for what is happening now on Earth, so you can plan your new lives with a view to helping humanity get back on track before it is too late. The biggest obstacle facing humans right now is the harm caused by the violence and strife that abounds throughout the planet, fueled by out-of-control toxic emotions. Humans must stop the abuse they heap on one another, on the other creatures who share the planet, and on Mother Earth herself.

"Does anyone have any questions at this time?"

A soul near the front of the stage spoke out: "Please refresh my memory about how this all started, and how I fit into the grand scheme of things."

"I will turn this over to Albert to answer," Sophia announced, as she motioned toward Albert. With a nod of his head to Sophia, Albert began his summary of how the universe came about.

# Chapter Two
## *Genesis*

"There was no beginning, and there will be no end. Eternity has no starting point and no finish line," Albert announced with conviction.

"The singularity of pure energy pulsated like a throbbing heart as it floated in the inky blackness of the void. This pinpoint of ethereal energy, which some humans refer to as the Source or the Creator, was self-aware and content with its state of existence.

"And then the Source decided to fill the empty space around it like an artist dabbing oil onto a blank canvas. It sent out plumes of energy in all directions, which rapidly fanned out from the Source to fill the void. Over time, the plumes of energy congealed into dense matter particles that eventually clumped together to form clouds of swirling gas. Aeons passed and this matter morphed into stars, planets, comets, nebulae, black holes, and everything else in our universe.

"The random interaction of energy and matter often produced primitive life forms that eventually evolved into the life forms that now populate Earth and numerous other planets in the universe.

"The Source was pleased with all it had created but wanted to experience the magnificence of the universe in all its intimate details. So, it created individual aspects of itself, little sparks of energy, to spin out from the Source to explore the universe. And because these scintillas of life, also known as souls, retained their connection to the Source, everything they encountered as they probed the wonders of the cosmos was also enjoyed by the Source.

"In order to better experience all the facets of the universe, these souls initiated the cycle of reincarnation into life forms on the denser planes as the means to face challenges and learn lessons available only on the lower dimensions. In this way they could grow, evolve, and accumulate wisdom in their quest to become more like the Source in every respect. The Source was pleased with this development, as it gave the Source an even greater appreciation of the vast diversity of energy, matter, and life in the universe it had created.

"All souls are on a never-ending journey of exploration, a trek with no timetables and no finish line. Everything they experience, whether incarnated into a physical life form or as beings of energy in the Spirit Realm, contributes to their evolution and growth as they move onward and upward at a pace they choose for themselves.

"The Source is the totality of everything in the universe. All things, whether animate or inanimate, are intimately connected to the Source and form part of its Divine Oneness. Each of you are one of its creations, and whatever you experience as a soul is also experienced by the Source. All the trials, tribulations, and triumphs that all souls have encountered since they spun out from the Source have been experienced by the Source, and this allows it to relish the diversity of feelings and consciousness in the life forms it created.

"All souls are individual aspects of the Source who were created to explore the universe in order to grow and evolve. And because each soul determines its own path for evolution and the things it chooses to experience, all soul journeys are different. Thus, all souls are unique in their own special way.

"The Source has not made any rules or guidelines for you to follow. Whatever you do during your incarnations in the physical world, or as a being of energy in the Spirit Realm, is neither good nor bad—it just is what it is. The Source has no expectations of you, and you cannot anger or disappoint the Source because everything you do is an expression of the sublime diversity created by the Source—a divine mélange of energy, vibration, and consciousness.

"The Source gave birth to the universe so it could enjoy the magnificence of what it was, a way to augment its self-awareness by admiring the ineffable splendor of the limitless cosmos it had spawned in that glorious moment of divine self-actualization.

"There is no analogy I can give you that will come close to explaining the majesty and mystery of this celestial opus. In human terms, it is like Da Vinci painting the Mona Lisa or Michelangelo sculpting David. They did so as a joyful expression of their unique abilities to capture the allure of the human journey on Earth. And when they had finished their masterpieces, they felt great pride in knowing what they had created would be admired by their fellow humans for years to come.

"The Source is the master architect of our vast cosmos, the prime mover of everything that exists in your observable universe, and all things beyond. The Source is the fountainhead of all love in the universe, and it projects its unconditional love to all things equally and without reservation. All its creations have their own special place in the grand scheme of things without any preferences or priorities."

"Who created the Source?" another soul asked.

"No one created the Source—it always was and always will be. The souls in the Spirit Realm accept this as a truism without hesitation, and whenever you cross over to the Spirit Side after completing an incarnation you will once again accept this truth as an unassailable reality."

"What is the purpose of my evolution? What am I trying to achieve, and when do I reach the end?" a soul near the front wondered.

"You want to grow and evolve to fulfill your destiny as a divine creation of the Source. You will continue to move onward and upward because that is the only direction you can go. Just as an acorn is destined to grow into an oak tree, you are destined to advance on a path of evolution without a finish line. Because the universe is constantly changing and expanding, you are on a never-ending journey of exploration and growth designed to help you to become more like the Source with each advance you make.

"And whenever you feel you are ready, you can merge back into the Source to enjoy the supreme ecstasy of divine love and perfect unity with the universe, before spinning out once more to continue your journey.

"All souls, whether incarnated in humans or animals on Earth or in alien life forms on other planets, are beings of pure energy—indestructible and eternal. They are on a voyage of exploration to experience the vast universe created by the Source in all its facets. Their goal is to grow and evolve to become more like the Source in every respect, and this is achieved by observing the interactions of energy and matter in the cosmos and by incarnating into the myriad of different life forms that inhabit the billions and billions of planets spread out among the countless stars in the heavens.

"Every soul began its journey when it spun out from the Source—like a spark of light from the Central Sun—while maintaining its intimate connection to the Source and to all the other souls who were already traversing the universe. Every adventure they experienced provided them with new knowledge and wisdom, much like how a blank canvas is turned into a masterpiece with deft brushstrokes by a creative artist. Every new experience adds another brushstroke to the story of their journey.

"The journey of the soul is a never-ending trek with no finish line, as each soul continually moves onward and upward. Each soul freely chooses the path it wants to follow, comforted by the knowledge there is no right or wrong track to follow. Every road traveled provides the soul with the experiences that allows it to grow and evolve. There are no wrong turns or dead ends, and they choose their own unique paths to follow.

"Souls can explore the universe by traversing in the high vibrations of the Spirit Realm, or they can choose to incarnate into life forms on the denser planes to get firsthand knowledge of life in low-vibration dimensions.

Most souls do choose to incarnate into such life forms because this is the best way to truly experience and understand life from the perspective of these lower echelon creatures.

"Planet Earth is one of these countless planets existing in the denser planes of the universe. Souls can incarnate into any of the creatures who inhabit Earth, including humans. Souls who are new to the Earth plane will often begin by incarnating into some of the simpler life forms, and then move up to the more complex lives enjoyed by humans. The life of a rabbit is much simpler to navigate than the convoluted lives enjoyed (or endured) by homo sapiens.

"As Sophia mentioned, the Earth school is one of the toughest schools in the universe, and it is not for the faint of heart. All humans living on Earth should pat themselves on the back for having the courage to take the plunge on this planet.

"So why do souls choose to incarnate on Earth instead of remaining on the Spirit Side? A good question because life on the Spirit Side is like living in paradise. Sophia, please describe life over here, so these good souls can fully appreciate what they will temporarily leave behind if they choose to incarnate on Earth."

# ❦ Chapter Three ❧

## *The Good Life*

Sophia glanced at Albert and continued the orientation: "A soul on the Spirit Side is a nonphysical being of pure energy that doesn't have to eat, drink, breathe, or procreate. There is no pain, suffering, or other hardships—only boundless happiness and bliss. And the Spirit Side has no negative emotions—only unconditional love for everyone no matter what they did since they spun out from the Source.

"On the Spirit Side, souls can instantly manifest anything they want merely by thought creation, because thoughts in the Spirit Realm are very powerful. The Spirit Side offers many exciting opportunities for souls to engage in numerous different forms of artistic, sporting, and recreational activities, including musical concerts by famous performers, live theater by renowned actors, and lectures by some of the most distinguished scholars to ever have walked the Earth. Attending a concert by the Beatles or Elvis, watching Richard Burton play the starring role in *Hamlet*, or listening to a lecture by Aristotle, are all examples of the never-ending cornucopia of exciting pursuits available to everyone without the need for tickets or reservations.

"Most Souls on the Spirit Side have projects they freely choose for themselves, but they don't have to do anything if that is their preference. Souls pursue various activities to increase their knowledge and evolve. Many souls assist other souls who are creating new Life Plans while others will help those souls who have recently crossed over become reacquainted with the Spirit Side. None of these activities is difficult or what you would consider work on Earth. Everyone does these things freely and with great love and joy.

"Souls do not have appointments or schedules on the Spirit Side. They can choose where they want to be and what they want to do without any concern about how much time they spend at each activity, since linear time does not exist on the Spirit Side. Even though humans consider a life span of eighty years to be a long time, it is only the 'blink of an eye' on the Spirit Side. A soul's incarnation on Earth does not result in a noticeable interruption of its activities on the Spirit Side, because the time spent during a life on Earth is relatively insignificant.

"As I mentioned, anything a soul wants it can create instantly by thought creation. Even though they have no real need for them, souls can create the things they enjoyed on Earth or wished they had been able to enjoy. A soul can thought create a huge mansion on a tropical island or a ski chalet in the mountains and live there until it no longer desires to do so. If a soul wants to go to another location, it can travel there instantly with thought creation, or it can create a red Ferrari and drive there. If a soul loved dining out in fine restaurants during its last incarnation, it can thought create gourmet restaurants and dine at them as often as it likes, even though they have no need to eat.

"Souls do not have a specific gender on the Spirit Side. Souls will often choose to appear to other souls in either the male or the female form, but this is a matter of personal preference for the soul. Souls can incarnate on Earth as either gender, and most souls will choose both sexes over the course of their lifetimes in order to experience all facets of life as a human.

"Every sporting and recreational activity humans' enjoy on Earth is available on the Spirit Side. Souls can downhill ski, surf, snorkel, parasail, kayak, hike, and climb mountains, to name a few, as well as all the indoor activities like bowling, squash, and billiards. You can watch theatrical plays, attend musical concerts, or enjoy sitting in the warm sunshine while cheering for your favorite baseball team. If you like, you can get together with friends for a chat over a beer.

"To expand your knowledge, you can attend lectures

given by famous professors and experts, arrange for private tutoring sessions on any topic you wish, or read books or watch videos by yourself in one of our libraries.

"There are no entrance fees or reservations required for any activity on the Spirit Side and never any waiting lines. If you get tired of the activities you remember from Earth, you can engage in all the different types of sports and recreation pursuits common on other planets, or you can invent new ones. There are no limits to the kinds of activities available to you, other than the limits of your own imagination.

"Boredom does not exist on the Spirit Side, because there are countless things to do and billions of stars and planets to explore. Souls will never be able to see or do everything in the universe even with the eternal lifespan they all enjoy. If a soul desires contrast to the never-ending array of interesting, amusing, and challenging activities on the Spirit Side, it can incarnate on one of the planets in the denser planes, such as Earth, to get a dose of the harsh conditions and difficult challenges that go with such a life. A soul who has returned from a difficult incarnation will appreciate the ecstasy of the Spirit Side even more than before.

"It is important to understand that when souls are in their natural form in the Spirit Realm, they do not have physical bodies. They are beings of energy that vibrate at a very high frequency, which means they can pass through matter on the denser planes like it wasn't there, and physical entities, like humans on Earth, cannot see or feel them because of their high vibrational rates. And because souls don't have physical bodies, they don't have sex organs and cannot engage in sexual intercourse like humans on Earth.

"As a result, sexual activities in the Earth sense do not happen on the Spirit Side. Quite often, however, two souls will choose to fuse their energies together for a few moments of sheer ecstasy. This is not for the purpose of procreation, but merely for the intense pleasure derived from this temporary union. There are no spouses or committed relationships on the Spirit Side, and thus these interactions do not breach any commitments or cause jealousy. These mergers between two souls happen freely and openly, and they never have any effect on other souls. Although souls do not have families in the Earth sense, they do belong to spirit groups that are like large, extended families.

"But do not be disappointed, because, as I mentioned before, souls on the Spirit Side have something much better than sex: it is a merging of energies between souls in what is known as the 'Dance of Heavenly Bliss.' Garnet, you had a chance to do this dance on one of your trips to the Spirit Side. Could you please tell us about this episode?"

"Certainly, Sophia," I responded. "On one of my trips with Albert, he introduced me to a soul named Votan, who stood before me as a handsome young man. (As you mentioned, Sophia, souls on the Spirit Side can choose how they appear to other souls, and so they will often manifest themselves as a male or female from one of their past lives on Earth, even though souls do not have a gender.)

"Votan explained we were part of the same soul group, and we had enjoyed many previous lives together on Earth. Quite often we were spouses, and sometimes he was the husband and other times he was the wife. He described our last life together on Earth during the height of the Mayan civilization in the city of Tikal. In that life he was a royal scribe, and I was a lady-in-waiting to the youngest daughter of the monarch. To make a long story short, it was love at first sight, and we went on to be married, living a long and happy life together.

"At this point Votan announced his primary purpose at this time was to show me what souls on the Spirit Side do when they desire a little ecstasy. What happened next, as set out in my third book, *Dance of Heavenly Bliss*, can best be described by quoting from a passage in chapter 27 of this book:

*Votan stood up and motioned for me to do likewise. Then without further ado, he stepped toward me and merged himself into my astral body. It felt like Votan and I had somehow fused our spirits into one clump of energy. My whole body tingled with a surge of divine love that left me aching with ineffable pleasure, as wave after wave of orgasmic euphoria rippled through my body in a rhapsody of sheer delight. Every atom of my body throbbed with a heavenly bliss that infused my whole being with unbridled exhilaration.*

*It was a dance of ecstasy—a joyous celebration of unity with another spark of energy. A dance choreographed by the Source to ensure the souls it created can enjoy the magnificence of its universe.*

*Time seemed to stand still as we danced in the eternal moment of Now. And then it was over when Votan took a step back to stand in front of me once again.*

"So, there you have it. The 'Dance of Heavenly Bliss' is an exhilarating dance of delight between two souls for the purpose of enjoying a few moments of sheer ecstasy. It is done openly, freely, and without any special attachment or commitment, and no prior consent is required or expected. To put it in perspective, imagine the best sex you can enjoy as a human on Earth, and then multiply that euphoria by a few thousand times, and you will come close to understanding what you will experience with the 'Dance of Heavenly Bliss.' Like I said to Votan after our dance was finished: 'I can hardly wait to do that again!'"

Albert chuckled at my recollection of this dance and said: "I remember watching you dance with Votan. I was amazed the dance lasted so long, given that you have two left feet and are tone deaf. And you did not seem to be uncomfortable doing this dance with Votan, who clearly presented himself as a male. Have you lost your heterosexual inhibitions about same-sex relationships?"

"Well, you know what they say: if you don't swing both ways you will miss half the action," I retorted, as Albert chortled with delight.

Sophia waved her arm impatiently and jumped in to put a stop to the blarney: "Thank you, Garnet, for that vivid recount of your experience with the 'Dance of Heavenly Bliss,' and now, if it is OK with you two blatherskites, I would like to continue my discourse about life on the Spirit Side.

"Souls on the Spirit Side exist on many different levels of advancement or evolution, based upon the knowledge and the wisdom they gained from previous incarnations. As I have said, souls can acquire knowledge on the Spirit Side in various ways, including reading books, watching videos, attending lectures, participating in discussion groups, and enjoying private sessions with the Wise Ones. Souls also learn a great deal from their life reviews after each incarnation and from watching other souls undertake their own life reviews. Souls can also learn much by acting as a spirit guide for another soul during one of its incarnations.

"Perhaps the best way for souls to learn is by exploring the universe—by traveling as spirits (without incarnating into physical bodies) to the stars and planets that exist in the denser planes of the universe. During these adventures, souls can learn a lot about the universe, and this knowledge will help them choose the planet for their next incarnation.

"Ultimately, most souls will choose to incarnate on the denser planes to experience the things they need in order to complete the knowledge they have acquired as spirits. The wisdom so gained from their lives on the denser planes allows them to accelerate their rate of evolution. Souls do not progress at the same pace—some are more advanced than others—but there is no hierarchy of souls in the Earth sense. All souls on the Spirit Side are equal, and the more advanced souls are not considered to be superior or better than the lesser advanced souls. It is like schools on Earth where high school seniors are not regarded as better than kindergarten students—just more advanced in their formal education. All souls continue to evolve—there are never any failures, and there are no timetables or deadlines to meet.

"Souls grow and evolve because that is the only direction they can go. Souls never go backward; they always move onward and upward. Souls evolve in order to become more like the Source in every respect, which is a moving target as the Source is constantly changing.

"There is no end to the levels of advancement for a soul and no finish line. The universe is infinitely vast with an infinite number of planes or dimensions that are always changing. Souls can never finish exploring and experiencing the universe since there is no end to the universe and its constant state of change. Every new experience in the universe provides souls with the opportunity to continue to grow and evolve in a never-ending process.

"The journey of the soul I have described is difficult for humans to comprehend fully, a fact you will have to deal with if you incarnate as a human on Earth. It is similar to a human trying to grasp the concepts of eternity and infinity, which cannot be understood completely due to the inherent limitations of the human mind. This is not unlike a person who has been blind since birth trying to understand color when he hears other people talk about the grass being green or the rose bloom having a bright red hue.

"Souls are ethereal beings of energy who eagerly pursue knowledge about the universe in all its dimensions by studying in the libraries that provide unlimited access to all the accumulated knowledge in the cosmos, and by accessing the Akashic Records to view the history of every life that has ever been lived in the universe.

"This 'book learning,' however, can only provide a limited scope of knowledge, and to complete and perfect their understanding of the universe and its life forms, souls must incarnate into creatures on the denser planes, like Earth, to get a 'hands-on' experience of life in those physical beings. A soul on the Spirit Side can observe the activities on Earth, but it won't truly understand what a human enjoys or endures during a life on Earth unless it incarnates into a human and encounters the events typically found in a journey on Earth.

"Physical pain and suffering, as well as fear, anger, hate, greed, do not exist in the Spirit Realm, nor does the joy from a romantic union, the birth of a child, or the achievement of a lofty goal. These physical and emotional sensations that happen frequently to the denizens of planet Earth cannot truly be experienced by reading a book, watching a video, or listening to a lecture—they can only be fully appreciated by incarnating into a physical body.

"I hope this explains why souls would leave the

blissful paradise on the Spirit Side to incarnate on Earth. It is the only way to complete their knowledge about life on Earth, and this firsthand experience allows them to grow and evolve as they continue their quest for knowledge and wisdom.

"Before we move on, I should forewarn you about the perception of time on the Earth plane, which is one of those elusive concepts that pervades all lives on Earth. Humans have come to understand that time progresses in a linear fashion from past to present to future, and they believe everything that has happened before the present is part of the past, and everything that will happen after the present moment is part of the future. This paradigm of how time unfolds governs their perception of the world and how they fit into it, but it is only an illusion on Earth, albeit a very persistent illusion.

"In reality there is no past or future, and everything happens in one big NOW moment that encompasses everything. So, all your 'past' lives and 'future' lives happen at the same time as your present lives. But to allow souls to enjoy the best learning experience from their lives on Earth, they are allowed to perceive them in sequence. So a life you lived in the fifteenth century appears to have preceded a life lived in the eighteenth century.

"Humans' perception of their lives in sequence could be described as a sequential concurrence or, if you like oxymorons, a concurrent sequence. And so you don't end up unduly interfering with the present life you are living, you are not allowed to view any of your 'future' lives until you perceive them in an orderly sequence.

"When your soul transitions to the Spirit Side after your physical body dies, you will be able to view all your 'past' lives in the Akashic Records, but you will not be able to view any of your 'future' lives, as this would interfere with the planning of your next incarnation.

"This concept of no linear time is very difficult for humans to grasp, because they must deal with the limitations of their puny human minds. Once back on the Spirit Side, souls will once again fully understand the concept of no linear time, and they will look with amusement at humans on Earth who are still reacting to things that happened in the past, or contemplating the future with eagerness or dread. In the meantime, while you are still completing your human journeys on Earth you will have to live with the grand illusion of linear time."

"Thanks for your explanation of why a soul would want to leave the splendor of the Spirit Realm to take the plunge on Earth," a soul in the upper level piped up. "I have made the decision to incarnate on this planet, so what is the next step?"

"Albert, I will hand this off to you, if you will,"

Sophia replied.

# ⁓ Chapter Four ⁓
## *Beginning the Cycle*

With a nod to Sophia, Albert stepped to the center of the stage and shared his wisdom with the crowd:

"All incarnations begin with the first step: the decision of a soul to continue its journey of exploration and learning by choosing a life as a human on Earth. Before doing so, a soul will be fully appraised of what life on Earth will be like, from firsthand experience from previous lives on this planet, by observing the activities on the planet from the vantage point of the Spirit Realm, and by discussions with other souls who have enjoyed previous incarnations on Earth.

"There are no accidental, capricious, or coerced incarnations on this planet. All decisions to take the plunge on the Earth plane happen only after a careful consideration of all the potential trials and tribulations the soul might encounter in the new life it is planning. And the final decision to incarnate is always totally up to the soul, without pressure of any kind from anyone.

"Once a soul has decided to take the plunge, the next

step is to prepare a Life Plan for its upcoming incarnation. All Life Plans set out the significant aspects of the proposed new life, including its place of birth, the first language learned, and the identity of its parents, siblings, friends, teachers, co-workers, and spouse. It might also set out some disability challenges the soul wants to encounter, such as blindness, deafness, deformity of limbs, mental illness, or other forms of mental or physical handicaps.

"The purpose of a Life Plan is to set the stage for the types of challenges and lessons the soul wants to encounter, so it can grow and evolve on its endless quest for knowledge and wisdom. And because all souls have traveled different paths since spinning out from the Source, they all have different needs to be fulfilled on their journeys on Earth.

"The development of a Life Plan is done through consensus. The soul proposing a Life Plan will consult with the souls who will play a major role in its upcoming life. They must agree to be part of the soul's new life, and the soul must agree to be part of their lives. Thus, the Life Plans of the soul and its main characters must mesh together by mutual agreement.

"In all planning sessions, a member of the Council of Wise Ones will review the Life Plan and make suggestions to ensure it is appropriate for the soul, based on what it wants to accomplish and its level of advancement. The Council wants to ensure a Life Plan is not too difficult for the soul, because a life filled with too many hardships or tragedies may cause a soul to give up and become depressed, thereby missing out on some learning challenges. On the other hand, a Life Plan setting out a soft and cushy life may be a wasted opportunity that will provide little growth. But in the final analysis, every soul makes the final determination of what will go into its Life Plan.

"Most souls belong to soul groups, and the members of a soul group will incarnate together on Earth in different roles to facilitate the journeys of every member of the group. In one life a soul may be the mother of a family while other members of the group will be the husband, son, daughter, uncle, aunt, or grandparent. And over all the incarnations, these roles alternate so a soul will experience lives as both sexes and in all the different roles, so it can encounter all aspects of a life on Earth.

"As mentioned earlier, the Council oversees all the incarnations on Earth, and one of their most challenging duties is providing guidance to souls who are preparing Life Plans for their incarnations on Earth. Life Plans are the cornerstone of every life and their importance cannot be overstated.

"As you heard, souls are on a never-ending voyage of exploration and growth—a trek with no finish line because our universe is constantly changing. It is a challenging journey all souls undertake joyfully with an unbridled zest for new adventures. There are no deadlines or timetables for this odyssey, and every soul gets to choose its own path for evolution.

"Souls who incarnate on Earth are at different stages of development. Some are new to the Earth school, many have lived hundreds of lives on this planet and are seasoned veterans, while most souls are somewhere in between. And to make matters even more interesting, prior to enrolling in the Earth school most of these souls have experienced a multitude of incarnations in a number of different life forms existing in our universe.

"All souls are unique in their own way because they have all had disparate experiences since they began their treks aeons ago, and it is this diversity of backgrounds that makes the Council's job so challenging. There are no cookie-cutter Life Plans they can pull off the shelf to offer to the souls about to embark on a journey on Earth. Every Life Plan must be carefully tailored to take into account the history and evolutionary goals for each soul.

"Those souls who have had numerous lives on Earth do not need much guidance from the Council because they are familiar with the perils and pitfalls common to a life on this planet. At the other end of the spectrum, however, the neophytes need a lot of hand holding when they prepare their Life Plans. All too often the newbies are keen to include too many daunting challenges for themselves in their upcoming life, and they would end up biting off more than they can chew unless the Council intervenes with a bit of sage advice.

"And there are many advanced souls who have already graduated from the Earth school who volunteer to fill roles in other people's lives to facilitate the challenges they need to encounter to further their growth. Without help from these Earth angels a lot of souls would drift aimlessly through their lives without making much progress.

"Once the Life Plan has been finalized, the next step is the descent of the soul to the denser planes to become joined with a human baby as it emerges from the birth canal. At this stage, many of the aspects of the Life Plan have already been established, such as the place of birth, the first language learned, and the identity of the soul's parents, siblings, and other relatives. But because humans do not remember what they included in their Life Plans, and as all humans have free will to act and make decisions, the rest of a soul's Life Plan is not etched in stone. The significant milestones and events the soul had hoped to achieve may or may not happen, depending on how that human, and the humans it interacts with on a day-to-day basis, exercise their free will. As a result, most humans will stray off course many times during their lifetimes.

"As I explained to you before, the usual pattern of human incarnation calls for a soul to enter a newborn infant at birth and reside in that body until it dies. I also told you every soul has the final decision on when to exit the incarnation and return to the Spirit Side. A soul's decision to terminate its journey on Earth is based on a number of factors, with the most important being an assessment of the progress it has made to learn the lessons it had planned before birth.

"Sometimes a soul will decide on an early exit if the life it chose was too difficult for it to endure in its current state of evolution. Or maybe the soul is just eager to return Home so it can plan another adventure on Earth in a new body.

"Typically, when a soul decides it is time to leave, it chooses an exit point—like an accident or disease—and it escapes when its body dies. But sometimes the soul will work out an exchange with another soul on the Spirit Side, so it will leave the physical body and the new soul, often called a 'walk-in,' will take its place. This happens when the incoming soul believes the body about to be abandoned would be a suitable vehicle for it to experience the things needed for its evolution. In other words, the incoming soul feels it doesn't need to start out as a baby and grow up into an adult, and its needs will be served by entering a mature body.

"Often this exchange is not noticed by the people close to the human in question, although occasionally it results in an inexplicable change in the personality and demeanor of the human who has received the new soul. Some people think the change results from a split personality, while others believe it is caused by illness or trauma. It is not easy for the new soul to fit into the new body without a few noticeable changes, and this can cause confusion and distress among its family members.

"The system works well for both souls. The soul wishing to exit is happy to accommodate the incoming soul because it has no further use for its human body, while the incoming soul can zero in on a life that will offer it the opportunities it needs without having to live through all the prior life events. The incoming soul will assume the remainder of the Life Plan that had been developed for that body by the outgoing soul, with amendments designed to focus on the needs of the new soul.

"When humans stare at their mugs in the mirror in the morning, they might ask the eternal question of life: Why am I here? And now you know the answer: Souls incarnate as humans to face the challenges and learn the lessons they hoped to encounter when they planned their incarnations.

"When you are having a journey on Earth, you

won't know exactly what you had hoped to encounter or accomplish in this life, because you will not be allowed to remember your life planning before you were born. There are, however, some universal principles you can follow to enjoy a happy and fulfilling journey on Earth. The most important of which is to embrace love and reject fear, the two polar opposites that are constantly battling for dominance in everyone's life.

"Fear, and all its toxic spin-off emotions, like anger, hate, greed, jealousy, and judging others, is the most caustic and destructive emotion on Earth. It is the cause of all the wars, genocide, terrorist acts, mass shootings, murders, and other criminal acts that have occurred with arduous regularity over the history of the planet.

"These negative emotions cause humans to fear and distrust other humans if they have a different color of skin, speak a different language, worship a different God, or have different customs, and this often leads to hate, anger, and violence. Greed and jealousy cause humans to resort to immoral or illegal appropriation of material goods or power from other people or countries, often through violence and oppression.

"Love, on the other hand, has no room for these toxic emotions, as it encompasses compassion, forgiveness, and acceptance for oneself and all others. Love recognizes that all humans are souls having a journey on Earth, and all souls are connected to each other and to the Source. As such, love enables everyone to embrace all other humans as individual aspects of the Source, as brothers and sisters in the cosmic family spawned by the Creator.

"When humans fully embrace love, the toxic emotions that plague their lives will wither away and die, along with the propensity to lash out violently in anger. Embracing love means forgiving others for their transgressions and never holding a grudge or seeking revenge. Love requires total acceptance of all others, regardless of their outward appearance or beliefs.

"No matter what challenges, lessons, obstacles, tragedies, or hardships you encounter, you know you will be on the right path if you react to them with love and stifle the temptation to let your negative emotions govern your actions. If you can do this, you will fulfill the goals of your soul, and speed your way toward graduation from this grueling school on the third rock from the Sun."

"Do we all have soul mates on Earth and is it our mission to meet with our soul mate before we die?" a soul in the top row inquired.

Albert nodded and responded: "The kind of relationship you have described happens often on the Earth plane, and it always arises between two people whose souls have lived previous lives together, often as spouses or lovers. Memories of these previous intimate relationships will leak through in a flash of recognition when they first meet, often evoking a feeling of déjà vu.

"It is like the revival of an ongoing passion that was interrupted briefly when they passed through the shroud of forgetfulness that is an integral part of the cycle of reincarnation. Its fervor is so strong it cannot be completely stifled by this cyclical amnesia, and it will percolate through to their human consciousness with mounting intensity.

"These individuals will not be able to recall the details of their previous lives together, but in their hearts they will feel a special attachment to each other that defies any plausible explanation. What starts out as love at first sight gradually matures into an enduring bond of friendship and intimacy that supersedes all other relationships—a union of divine energy in a world plagued by illusions of separation.

"When you notice these couples on Earth, you will sense their special connection, and you will notice how they seem to know what each other is thinking without verbal communication, and they will often finish each other's sentences. And if one is in distress, the other will know something is wrong even though they are separated by hundreds of miles.

"Because souls tend to travel in soul groups for their incarnations on Earth, a person's soul mate is usually a member of this troupe, but not necessarily the same soul over the course of all lives on your planet. Soul mates change over time due to the complex interaction of souls over numerous lifetimes.

"You should know, however, not everyone on Earth has a soul mate living on the planet. Quite often one of the souls in the coupling will choose not to incarnate in one of the cycles for reasons pertaining to its evolution, and the Earth-bound soul will have to eke out a life on its own until they are reunited once again on the Spirit Side.

"When you have incarnated on Earth and haven't found your soul mate, do not despair because maybe it was not intended for you to connect in this life. And if you do find your special person you will know it immediately, and you should skip down the road shouting 'hallelujah' at the top of your lungs.

"So far we have been talking about human incarnations. What about the other creatures who share the planet? Do animals have souls? You need only look into the eyes of any dog, cat, or other pet to find the answer. It is obvious animals do have souls, just like humans, and they are all having a journey on Earth as part of their evolution.

"In fact, many humans have enjoyed previous lives as animals, a thought that is disturbing to a lot of people. For some, the thought they might reincarnate as an animal is distressing, because they look at the lives of animals as inferior to humans and, in many cases, as lives filled with abuse and terror. But that is viewing those lives from a human perspective, which assumes it would be a horrible existence to endure the life of one of the creatures who share our planet.

"Souls on the Spirit Side do not view things in that way. They understand much can be learned from a life as an animal, with more simplicity and joy than the complicated lives of humans. Animals are naturally more aligned with Mother Earth, which allows them to be more appreciative of the beauty of nature. And animals don't have to worry about making mortgage payments, saving for retirement, or finding a job they really like. The uncomplicated nature of their lives permits animals to focus on the present moment, because they are not burdened with thoughts of the past or concerns about what the future may bring.

"You should not be concerned about potential animal incarnations, because the choice of lives is always totally up to the soul. If a soul does not want to incarnate as an animal, no one will force it to do so, which should be comforting to those humans who shudder at the thought of coming back as a rabbit or a snake. In many cases, souls who are new to the Earth plane will incarnate initially as animals in order to get their feet wet on this planet, and then move up to the much more complicated lives as humans. Although human souls can reincarnate as animals, most will not do so because such lives would be too easy to navigate and not much would be learned.

"And it is not just animals on Earth that have souls, but all the life forms on the billions and billions of planets in the universe also have souls like human souls. When you return to the Spirit Side after your human life is over, you can freely choose to incarnate into an alien life form anywhere in the cosmos, as you are not restricted in any way to planet Earth.

"Armed with this knowledge, all humans should look at animals in a different light and do their best to treat them with the dignity and respect they deserve, because they all have their own rightful place in the universe."

"The fact that souls who incarnate on Earth will not remember where they came from, or what is in their Life Plans, is one of the main reasons this school is so difficult," Sophia chimed in. "But souls are not left to flounder totally in the dark, as every soul will have several spirit guides to help them find the right path.

"Albert, would you be good enough to tell us about spirit guides?"

# ᯓ Chapter Five ᯓ
## *Guidance from Heaven*

Albert stepped to center stage and addressed the crowd:

"The good news is that everyone receives guidance on a regular basis from their spirit guides, who are like life coaches from the Spirit Realm. Everyone has several guides who are chosen before the soul incarnates, and although one or two will be with the person from birth to death, others will come and go to fit the needs of the soul as it progresses on its human journey.

"Spirit guides are constantly on duty, 24/7, and the messages they send to us are intended to guide us on the path we had hoped to follow in our Life Plans. Their messages are usually not direct telepathic communications, but are much more subtle, like intuitive thoughts, gut feelings, whispers in our minds, and coincidental events. As a result, most humans do not hear these messages or do not understand where they are coming from. And then quite often the human mind will convince the human to ignore the message, or it will propose a course of action contrary to the wise counseling from their spirit guides.

"All this makes it difficult for humans to follow the guidance they get from the Spirit Realm, and it is a very significant challenge humans face on planet Earth. But why not allow spirit guides to communicate directly with humans and provide them with the details of their Life Plans? Because to do so would make things too easy, and not much would be learned. It would be like a teacher giving her students the questions and answers to a final exam before the exam.

"The challenge for humans is to become better listeners, so they can hear, understand, and act on the directions they get from their guides. The best way to develop keener listening skills is through meditation, which helps to quiet one's mind and get rid of the clutter of thoughts that churn through a person's mind every day. When a quiet mind is achieved, the messages from the guides will come through with much more clarity, and the ability to follow this guidance will help to make a human journey more fulfilling.

"Everyone should be comforted to know no one is ever alone—your spirit guides will always be with you, even if you are not aware of their presence. And at the end of the day, when your physical bodies die, your guides will be waiting for you to leave your lifeless vessels so they can lead you back home to the Spirit Side.

"Most spirit guides have lived on Earth themselves, so they can appreciate what you are going through and the difficulties you will endure. Most often, your spirit guides are part of your spirit group, and they have lived in a close relationship with you in past lives.

"The main duty of your spirit guides is to give you guidance when you come to a fork in the road and must make a decision. At these junctures, your spirit guides will send you messages to encourage you to take the right path—the path intended in your Life Plan—except you do not always hear or understand their messages because your mind is too cluttered with other thoughts. Often, they send their messages in the form of an intuitive thought or feeling that suddenly pops into your head, and sometimes they are embedded in one of your dreams. At other times, you might receive guidance in the form of verbal statements made by other people (who are prompted by their spirit guides) or through the occurrence of 'coincidental' events in your life. These messages are easy to miss unless you watch for them and take the time to decipher their meaning.

"Whenever you get an intuitive thought or feeling (like a whisper in your mind), make sure you pause, listen carefully, and try to understand what it is trying to tell you. Most often, it is a message from your spirit guides. Frequently, your mind will ignore the whisper or rationalize a different course of action, but you must resist these tendencies and be more vigilant at following the guidance in these messages.

"Practicing meditation will help you hear these messages as it will calm your mind and clear out all the thoughts you will usually have swirling around in your mind. There is a long history of religious and spiritual men and women using meditation as a way to connect with their 'Higher Selves' and the universe. Meditation can help you open the channels of communication with your spirit guides so you will be able to hear and understand more of the messages you receive every day from the Spirit Side. As an added benefit, meditation can relieve your stress and help you face your day-to-day struggles with a more serene outlook."

"I have a question for you, Albert," a soul said from the far right of the arena. "Based on my research, it seems more and more people are reporting communications with deceased loved ones from this side of the veil. Is the veil getting thinner, as some claim, or is it because people are not as fearful of going public with these experiences as they were in the past? Can you shed any light on this?"

Albert looked pensive as he gathered his thoughts to respond: "The veil that divides the Earth plane from the Spirit Realm is a mutable shroud that is constantly shifting and swirling around all living things on the denser planes.

The ability of such creatures to peer through the veil to see spirits on the other side depends on their state of consciousness and their willingness to accept the reality of life beyond the veil.

"And I am not just talking about humans on the planet. Animals can also peer through the veil to varying degrees, even though they usually can't verbalize these episodes. People who own cats or dogs will often notice that their pets seem to be seeing and hearing things humans cannot detect, such as when they stare intently at something in what appears to be an empty room, or when they bark or meow excitedly for no apparent reason. In most of these cases, they are viewing spirits from the other side that are undetected by their owners.

"In the case of humans, a few can peer through the veil with relative ease, while to others the veil is an impenetrable curtain. People who have expanded their consciousness and raised their vibrations find it easier to penetrate the veil than those who are mired in unhealthy emotions, which slows down their vibrations and impedes their ability to fully perceive the reality of their existence.

"And your beliefs will either enhance or restrict your ability to peer through the veil. If you believe all souls are eternal and your deceased loved ones have crossed over to the other side, you will readily accept and understand the signs that are sent to you from the Spirit Realm. And the more you accept, the more you will perceive.

"On the other hand, if people have closed their minds to the possibility of life after death, or if they have subscribed to the teachings of some religions that the souls of dead people cannot communicate with the living because of an impenetrable barrier between Heaven and Earth, they will not recognize these signs as communications from the Other Side. Humans tend to believe what they have been conditioned to believe, and everything else is shunted to the side and ignored.

"The tidings from the Spirit Realm can take different forms; sometimes it will be as simple as a white feather appearing out of nowhere, a loved one's favorite song playing unexpectedly on the radio, or a vision in a dream. In a few situations, the recipient may get to see the ethereal apparition of someone they miss. No matter what the form, those people who believe in the reality of the afterlife will understand that someone from the other side of the veil is connecting with them to provide confirmation they are alive and well in a beautiful and peaceful place.

"To get back to your question, the veil is becoming thinner for enlightened people, but it is still an impervious shroud for those who still live in the fog of spiritual illiteracy. And the marked increase in reports of spirit communication results from this thinning of the veil and greater public acceptance of this phenomenon in recent years."

"The process of getting into a body for a human journey seems fairly straightforward," this soul noted. "But what about the process of dying? Will the transition back to the Spirit Side be easy or difficult?"

Sophia stepped forward to field this question after Albert motioned it was her turn.

# ⁓ Chapter Six ⁓
## *Transition to Paradise*

"This is a good question, and one of concern to any soul planning an incarnation on Earth," Sophia responded. "We all know death on Earth is inevitable, whether due to 'old age,' a terminal disease, or a tragic event. But who determines how and when a human body will perish? Is the end date dictated by the Source or the Grim Reaper? The short answer is that a person's soul determines when to exit the incarnation, without any interference from the Source or anyone else.

"Every soul includes several potential 'exit points' in its Life Plan, and as its life progresses on Earth it can decide which exit it wants to use to leave the incarnation. And these exit points can be changed by the soul after it has incarnated, just as a soul can modify its Life Plan from time to time during the incarnation.

"This means no one dies by accident. We leave our incarnations when our souls decide it is time to go, even though our human minds are not consciously aware of our souls' decision in this regard. If a plane crashes, killing all three hundred people on board, these deaths were not accidental, because the souls of each and every one who died in the crash had decided to use this tragedy as an off ramp for their incarnation. Souls make these decisions based on what they have experienced so far in their lives and what they might further accomplish, if anything, by continuing the incarnation.

"Once the soul has made its decision on how and when to exit, events start to unfold to fulfill this desire. Cancer begins to develop, heart or lung disease starts to form, or it is arranged for the human to be at the wrong place at the wrong time for a fatal accident to occur. No matter how the death happens, it is always at the behest of the soul even though the human desperately pleads for more time. It is natural for humans, and their loved ones, to want to beat the Grim Reaper as long as possible, but the soul is undeterred by such entreaties because it knows what is best for its continued growth and evolution. And since your human minds will not be privy to these exit points, and you will not be aware of what your souls are planning for you, the whole concept of preplanned exits may seem very strange to you, although it should give you great comfort to know you will not perish as a result of some random event before your soul is ready to end its journey on Earth.

"And now you might be wondering how souls always

get to choose their exit points, given that the world is full of humans who are exercising their right to take free will actions, often in unpredictable ways, and the random effect of natural disasters on the planet, like earthquakes, hurricanes, floods, and wildfires.

"The answer is very simple: all people on Earth have guardian angels whose job it is to protect them from physical death when their souls are not ready to leave. Angels are spirits who dwell in the Spirit Realm as special aspects of the Source. Their mission is to help souls get the most out of their incarnations on the denser planes, and they do so in many ways. Some have been given names by humans, like the Archangels referred to in the scriptures, but most exist happily in obscurity as they carry out their labor of love.

"Angels usually do not incarnate into physical entities, but sometimes they will manifest themselves in physical form on Earth when it is necessary to achieve their goals. Their usual modus operandi is to provide inspirational thoughts and intuitive messages to people to guide them in the right direction. In this way, they act in coordination with your spirit guides to provide guidance when needed.

"One of the most important roles for an angel is to act as a 'guardian angel' for someone on Earth. Every human has one or more guardian angels to watch over them and try to steer them away from potential danger. In the midst of the oft-chaotic frenzy of life on Earth, where your own free actions must interact with the free will actions of other humans, tragic events may result in untimely physical harm or death at a time when your soul is not ready to leave the incarnation. In these cases, your guardian angel with step in to prevent such a death or serious injury so your life will not end before your soul is finished with the incarnation.

"Angelic intervention is usually very subtle, and most often goes unnoticed by humans. For example, if you were scheduled to be on a flight that will crash and kill everyone on board, they will send strong intuitive messages to you to book a different flight (which you will do based on a 'hunch' you suddenly had to make a change). If this doesn't work, they can physically intervene to ensure you don't board the flight—like causing a traffic jam to hold you up on the way to the airport. When people realize they have narrowly averted death, they will often chalk it up to luck, but in most cases it was their guardian angel working behind the scenes to avert tragedy. Everyone should take comfort in knowing these angelic beings are always watching over us to ensure you don't die until your time is up.

"So, what happens when someone does die in a car accident? Was her guardian angel asleep? Your guardian angels are always watching over you, and when someone dies in an accident her guardian angel let it happen because that person's soul wanted to use the accident as an exit point.

"And what happens when a soul leaves a human body to transition to the Spirit Side? Typically, the transition is easy and painless, and most often the soul exits the body just prior to the final death throes. If your destiny is to die in a car crash, your soul will leave your body prior to the impact, and you will feel no pain or discomfort from the collision. Your soul would hover over the scene and watch the final moments with cool detachment, as you would realize the body you occupied for so long was merely a vehicle for your journey on Earth, and it is no longer needed.

"When your soul leaves your body, it will be met by your spirit guides who will gently guide you back to the Spirit Side. There you will encounter your welcoming party who will wrap you in warm hugs and unconditional love. Usually a welcoming party will include your deceased loved ones, and sometimes one or more of your favorite pets will join the group. All in all, it will be a wonderful, uplifting experience you should all look forward to with great anticipation.

"Once back on the Spirit Side you will recall all the details of your Life Plan and all the things you hoped to encounter in the life you just left. And when you are ready, you will have a Life Review with the able assistance of your spirit guides. During your Life Review, you will be able to review everything you said or did, and all the events that happened to you, in great detail. You can watch the replay of your life like a 3-D movie, in chronological order or in any sequence you desire. As you look back on your life, you will also be able to hear the thoughts and feel the emotions of the people you interacted with on planet Earth. If you said some mean and hurtful words to a co-worker, you will feel their pain and shame as they listened to your tirade, not knowing why you were unleashing your anger at them. And you will discover all the times you hurt or offended someone when you didn't intend to do so, which will drive home the lesson that you should always be careful about what you say and do.

"On the other hand, you will also be able to feel the love and gratitude from those people who you helped in some way. You will get the full and complete picture of all the good and bad things you did, whether intentionally or not.

"You must understand your Life Review is not something you will undergo as punishment for your hurtful actions or to make you feel bad about yourself. It is intended to be a learning tool to help you understand how your actions affected others, so you can plan to do better in your next incarnation. Your guides will help you grasp the significance of your actions and provide sage advice on how you could have avoided some of the pitfalls you stumbled into that caused you or those around you to be inflicted with unnecessary suffering.

"When your Life Review is finished, you will then be free to enjoy your sojourn in paradise, frolic with your soul group, plan your next incarnation (if you choose to incarnate again), or explore the universe as a nonphysical being. There are no restrictions or timetables for your evolution, and you get to decide for yourself what to do next.

"Many people on Earth have personally experienced the tragic death of a child or have learned about such tragedies happening to others. One of the worst things that can happen to a parent is the death of a child, especially a young child who has their whole life ahead of them. There is nothing more tragic and heart-wrenching than your six-year-old daughter being struck and killed at a crosswalk—a beautiful little girl who was loved by everyone and a joy to be around. How could God let this happen? you may demand.

"First, you must realize God (Source) does not make things happen or prevent things from happening on Earth. So, it was not the Source's decision that this mishap should occur, because the Source does not manipulate or control events on the planet. As previously stated, what happens to us on Earth is the result of our prebirth planning, our own free will actions, and the free will actions of the other people in the world.

"Although I mentioned that souls establish their exit points as part of their prebirth planning, you may wonder why a soul would go to the trouble of incarnating on Earth for only a few short years? What could possibly be learned in such a short life?

"There is always a good reason for a soul to incarnate as a human, but the reason a soul would choose a short life is not always the same. In some cases, a soul needs only a few years in a human incarnation to learn the lessons it needs to further its evolution, and then it is free to move on to other challenges.

"In other situations, an advanced soul who no longer needs to learn anything from life on Earth may choose a short life with a tragic ending solely to help other souls learn the lessons and face the challenges they need for their growth. As an example, the soul of the little girl killed in the crosswalk may have agreed to incarnate into that girl as a service to the souls of her parents, who needed to deal with the challenge of having their child die at a very young age. Such events often end up with the parents blaming each other for her death, resulting in a breakup of their marriage or with one of them spiraling down into the depths of despair. In such a case, the parents, as part of their prebirth planning, would have recruited the soul of the little girl to play a crucial role in their upcoming lives—a role designed to test the parents' ability to handle the tragedy without falling apart.

"If such a horrible mishap happens to you or someone you know, do not despair or become angry with the Source, because it happened as part of the grand scheme of incarnations designed to test the mettle of souls who dare to incarnate on planet Earth. And do not feel sorry for the little girl, because her soul will be back on the Spirit Side enjoying the bliss that awaits us all after we leave our physical bodies behind."

"What about suicide, Sophia?" someone in the second row inquired. "How does it fit into the scheme you just described?"

"Another good question," Sophia acknowledged. "Many souls wonder about using suicide as an exit point if things become too difficult during an incarnation, and I will do my best to give you guidance on this much-debated topic."

# ᘒ Chapter Seven ᘒ
## *Never Give Up*

"Historically, most societies abhor suicide, and most religions consider it a grave sin," Sophia continued. "But is suicide contrary to the laws of the Source? Is it possible for a soul to include suicide in its Life Plan?

"Suicide, like everything else that happens on Earth, is not inherently wrong. The Source does not punish anyone for committing suicide just as it does not punish souls for anything else they do in their lives.

"Most societies regard suicide as the cowardly act of desperate individuals unwilling to persevere with the life the Source created for them. Suicide is viewed as a sin because it is thought to thwart the plans the Source has made for these individuals. Historically, however, a few societies did not regard suicide as being universally bad. For example, in Roman times a disgraced citizen was expected to do the honorable thing and fall on his sword. In feudal Japan, samurai warriors who were about to be captured were expected to die with honor by committing seppuku, a ritualized form of suicide.

"On the Spirit Side, suicide is discouraged when it is used as an escape from the hardships and difficulties people might face in their lives, because often these circumstances were challenges their souls had wanted to experience when they created their Life Plans. In many of these cases, these individuals are blocking all positive messages from their spirit guides and refusing to accept that they have created their own reality. Quite often, they believe they are victims who have been treated harshly and unfairly by the universe and have no hope for a better future. And sometimes individuals commit suicide as an act of revenge to hurt other people, especially family members, for their previous hurtful actions.

"Even though people who commit suicide are not punished for doing so, in most cases it results in partially wasted lives because they missed some of the important challenges they had hoped to face. Once back on the Spirit Side, these souls will realize they need to return to Earth in another life to try again. On rare occasions, it is possible for a soul to include suicide as an exit point in its Life Plan.

"Chronic depression is a debilitating disease that zaps all goodness and hope from life. It is important to seek medical help and never feel embarrassed about disclosing your condition to your physician. And let friends and family know what you are going through because they can be there for you when you need it the most.

"The most important thing is to understand there is always hope no matter how faint it appears to be. Once you understand you are an eternal being who will return to the Spirit Side after the death of your human body, the troubles you will be facing on Earth will be more bearable if you know they will not last, and you will not take them with you. The challenges you face on Earth are temporal and, no matter how many mistakes you make, you will always return Home. You can never become lost.

"You cannot escape from your plight by taking your own life, because your desire to grow and evolve as a soul will dictate that you will continue to include these hurdles in your future incarnations until you have conquered them all. It is best to fight your way through these difficulties now so you can move on to other challenges in your evolution.

"And you have to understand you are not a victim of a capricious god who is making your life miserable. You are the author of your own story by virtue of your prebirth planning and your free will actions. If you don't like how your story is playing out, then rewrite your script by changing your reactions to the events in your life. Look at every hardship as a learning experience—an opportunity for growth.

"You must remember you are never alone, even if you

feel abandoned and misunderstood by family and friends. You have spirit guides who are there for you every step of the way. They are loyal friends who shower you with unconditional love even when you don't hear or follow their advice. They are the best friends you will ever have, and you only need to sit quietly in meditation to feel their presence and hear their guidance. They have been with you since birth and they will be there when you leave this life to guide you back Home. Follow their guidance and you will have a much happier journey on Earth.

"If a person is contemplating a suicide that is not a Life Plan exit point, their spirit guides will try to persuade the person to hang in there, usually by coaching via embedded messages during the individual's sleep and dream states.

"Sleep is a 'time out' for the body and mind, as well as the soul. Life on Earth is not easy; it is full of discomfort, pain, and hardships. On the physical level, sleep allows the body to be at rest to allow for growth and rejuvenation. For the mind, it is a period when it can shut down and block out the constant barrage of physical and emotional data it receives while awake, thus providing a respite from the turmoil caused by analyzing and reacting to this information.

"Most importantly, sleep allows a soul to escape from its human body and journey to the Spirit Side. Since a soul experiences everything its human encounters in its life, it needs a periodic break from this action to give it the opportunity to reflect on the events of the day. When a soul leaves the body during sleep, it goes to the Spirit Side to meet with its spirit guides and other souls in its spirit group. It will discuss the recent events in its life and review the upcoming schedule in its Life Plan. Its spirit guides will give it advice and loving encouragement.

"It is similar to a football game on Earth. At half-time, the players leave the field to go into the locker room where they can relax and rest their tired bodies. Their coaches will review the plays of the first half and offer suggestions on how they might have avoided their mistakes. They will give the team a pep talk in order to send them back onto the playing field with a positive attitude.

"Similarly, when people are asleep, their souls will listen to the advice of their spirit guides and reflect on what has happened so far in their lives. Quite often their souls will adjust their Life Plans based on this guidance.

"Because everything is so pleasant on the Spirit Side, a soul is often reluctant to return to its body in the morning for another day on Earth, and it is eager to return to the Spirit Side each night, which influences the actions and tendencies of the human it occupies.

"When your human is born and your soul first enters your body, the whole ordeal will be unpleasant and challenging. Remember you came from the Spirit Side and life on Earth is quite harsh in contrast. At this early stage of your life, your soul will need more time out of your body than it does when you are more mature, and that is why you will spend more time sleeping when you are a baby. As you grow older, your soul will became more accustomed to being in your body and putting up with the hardships, and it will have less need to escape.

"I hope this sheds some light on the role suicide plays in the cycle of reincarnation on Earth. Are there any questions at this point?"

A soul at the back of the stadium stood up and said: "How does the Source fit into this picture? Does the Source dictate the details of our incarnations or affect the circumstances of our lives?"

"We always get this question in our orientation sessions," Sophia replied. "I will let Albert respond to this one."

# ≈ Chapter Eight ≈
## *What about God?*

Albert took his cue and addressed the audience:

"What role does the Source play in the lives and happenings on Earth? Does the Source manipulate and control events on Earth? Does it make rules for us to follow? Will the Source judge souls in the afterlife, and reward or punish them based on what they did during their lives? These are all good questions, and the answers might surprise some people.

"Contrary to what many religions preach, the Source (or God) does not manipulate events on Earth. The Source is a passive observer of all the things that happen in the universe it created, and it does not interfere in any way. Just as the Source will not choose the life you will have on Earth or force you to incarnate, the Source does not intercede in how your life plays out in your human journey.

"If a natural disaster or a personal tragedy happens in your life, it should not be blamed on the Source. Likewise, if you are blessed with success and good fortune, it was not the Source that arranged for these gifts to be bestowed upon you or your family. What happens to you on your human journey is the result of the life you planned before you were born, your free will actions and decisions, and the free will actions of the other humans you will interact with on a regular basis.

"You are the author of your own play, and you will continually rewrite the script as you make your way through life. Your reaction to the events you encounter, whether good or bad, creates your reality, and all this happens without any manipulation by the Source.

"Praying to God to cure a disease, or help you pass an exam, find a new job, or meet a new life partner is a fruitless exercise, because the Source will not intervene, regardless of whether or not you have worshipped God in accordance with the rules and beliefs of your religion.

"The good news, however, is the Source does not make rules for souls to follow, a concept that flies in the face of what religious holy men have been preaching for centuries. The mainstream religions tell us God has made rules for us to follow, and if we breach these rules we will be punished in the afterlife. These rules encompass a broad spectrum of conduct, including how to treat your fellow humans and how to worship and pay proper homage to God and his earthly servants.

"Although the rules that dictate treating other humans with dignity and respect are inherently good and worthy of adherence by everyone, they did not come from the Source but were developed by humans to promote a safe and happy society. The rules that dictate how and where a person must worship God were developed by holy men to control the masses through guilt and fear, so they could further their own agendas to gain power and wealth. These holy men managed to convince their followers that all the rules they promulgated came from God, thus giving them unquestionable credence. And then to ensure obedience, they decreed that anyone who breached these rules (and did not make amends) would suffer eternal damnation.

"And thus fear became the main tool for them to gain power and control over the masses. Fear of eternal damnation helped to fill the church pews every Sunday, giving them a captive audience to listen to their self-righteous sermons and fill the collection plate with donations they needed to further their agendas. The fiction that God made the rules they disseminated to their followers, and the prospect of eternal damnation for disobedience, was essential to their goal of expanding their base of adherents and increasing the flow of donations, thereby giving them even more power and control.

"As stated before, the Source does not make rules for souls to follow, and the views to the contrary are nothing more than an insidious charade perpetrated on naïve people over the history of humankind. It follows that if the

Source does not make rules for souls to follow, it does not judge them in the afterlife, and it does not punish souls for their deeds or misdeeds during their lives on Earth. There is no one who will judge you when you cross over, except yourself, and places of punishment, like Hell, simply do not exist. Hell is another fiction created by holy men to instill fear and obedience in their flocks.

"At the end of the day, every soul returns to the Spirit Side when their physical bodies die, regardless of how they lived their lives, because there is nowhere else to go. This means, of course, that murderers and terrorists return to the Spirit Side, just like Mother Teresa. Souls return to the Spirit Side as that is their true home, and the place from which they can assess the lives they completed to understand how their journeys unfolded when compared to their Life Plans.

"Although this concept will seem unfair and unjust to many humans (because they feel bad people should be punished in the afterlife), it is the true reality of the cycle of reincarnation on Earth—like it or not. Souls on the Spirit Side have no difficulty whatsoever understanding this reality, because from that perspective they can see the big picture without being obscured by the fog of human consciousness.

"If the Source does not dictate the lives souls must live and does not interfere with the happenings on Earth, what is the role of karma? Are souls bound to continue their lives on Earth until they have balanced out their negative karma?

"Karma does not bind souls helplessly to a series of incarnations they must undergo until they have been purged clean of previous transgressions. Karma is not a universal law that must be adhered to by all souls. Rather, it is a way to measure the good deeds against the bad deeds so a soul can assess where it stands after any lifetime. Every soul has a strong moral imperative to act out of love, and not fear, in all its lifetimes, and this compels souls to freely choose to reincarnate again and again until they rid themselves of any negative karma they have accumulated.

"The decision to reincarnate is entirely up to the soul, without any coercion or undue influence from anyone else. And should a soul choose to never return to the Earth plane even when they have racked up negative karma, they are free to do so without any feelings of guilt or remorse.

"Karma does play a role in where a soul chooses to incarnate and what is included in its Life Plan. For example, a soul who physically abused his children in one life might choose to come back as a child who will be abused by his father, so the soul can truly appreciate the pain and suffering of an abused child. Or, a soul who lived a life of wealth and luxury and was cruel to less fortunate humans may choose a life as a penniless peasant in order to understand the hardships experienced by people living in poverty.

"And in one graphic example recounted by Dolores Cannon when regressing one of her clients who had been blind since birth, the client stated she had been a cruel tyrant in a previous life who liked to poke out the eyes of her prisoners. The soul of that tyrant chose to incarnate as a blind person so it could fully comprehend what it was like to function as a sightless human.

"In many cases karma can also be balanced through positive deeds in a future life. A soul who lived a life as a drug addict, stealing from others to pay for his drugs, may choose a life of a social worker who toils relentlessly to help downtrodden drug addicts kick the habit.

"Karma is not a punishment inflicted on a soul who committed misdeeds in previous lives. It is an opportunity for the soul to plan future lives to see what it is like to be on the receiving end of abuse, to ensure it would not repeat the same mistakes in a future life. Or past karma may encourage a sole to plan a life where it can purge previous transgressions by living a life of grace and making a positive impact on society.

"So why can't we remember our past lives? It would be very useful to help us understand how we accumulated negative karma so we can avoid the same mistakes in the current life. This reality is very frustrating for those people who understand they have lived before; however, there is a good reason for this temporary amnesia during your journeys on Earth.

"If you remembered all your past lives, it would be a difficult burden for you to carry in your current life. You would remember all the bad things you had done in previous lives, as well as all the physical and emotional pain you had suffered at the hands of other people. These memories would be very distressful, and you would spend too much time trying to deal with your guilt for your past misdeeds or your anger or sadness for the hurtful actions of others. These memories would be distracting, and they would interfere with your ability to live your life according to your Life Plan.

"As well, if you could recall the happiness and love you enjoyed on the Spirit Side before you were born, it would be more difficult for you to continue your journey as planned. Life on Earth is not easy because it is a difficult school. If you remembered how wonderful the Spirit Side was, and you knew you would return there after you died, it would be very tempting for you to hasten your return by taking your life. This could end your incarnation before you had a chance to encounter everything your soul had planned when it created your Life Plan.

"Finally, as I mentioned before, any recollection

of the details of your Life Plan would prejudice your adventure since you would know in advance what events were likely to happen and how you were supposed to react to them.

"Sometimes a few of these past-life memories will leak through to a human mind, either directly or subconsciously. In these cases, the ability of a person to access such memories usually results from a concerted effort by the person's spirit guides to open channels of awareness to assist in advancing the individual's Life Plan agenda.

"There are numerous examples of this. The most common one is the feeling of déjà vu many people have had at one time or another. Often this occurs when they travel to a place for the first time and get a strange feeling they have been there before, because the surroundings seem familiar. In most of these cases, they are accessing a residual memory of a previous life when they lived in that particular locality.

"In a few cases, memories of a past life show through in a new life as flashes of musical or artistic talent, especially in child prodigies. Mozart began composing music when he was five, an age when most other children are playing with toys. Most likely he was able to access memories of a previous life as a musician and composer, and thus he got a head start in his new incarnation.

Often souls who have dedicated their lives on Earth to a particular pursuit will reincarnate as a person who can continue this passion in another life. Sometimes young children will be able to describe the details of a place they have never visited before and/or understand a language they have never been exposed to in their current lives. These children are remembering places and events from a previous life.

"On the negative side, past-life memories can trigger fears or phobias in humans. Those individuals who have a fear of water might be accessing a residual memory of drowning in a previous life. People terrified of heights may have fallen to their deaths in another life. Occasionally, these residual memories of events from a past life result in physical anomalies in a person's current life. A person with a medically inexplicable painful leg might be tapping into a memory of a previous life as a soldier during World War I, when he died from a gunshot wound to his thigh.

"For the most part, however, souls remember very little of their previous lives so they can enjoy their journeys unencumbered by guilt or remorse from their previous lives on the denser planes."

"If the Source does not manipulate or control events on Earth, how do you explain the 'miracles' that have been chronicled in the Bible and other holy scriptures?" another soul asked.

"The miracles you refer to, like Jesus walking on water, turning water into wine, and raising people from the dead, actually did happen—but they were not caused by the Source," Albert explained. "Instead, the miracles performed by Jesus resulted from his ability to focus his thoughts into powerful beams of energy that affected matter and energy in ways that defied logical explanations based on the science of the time.

"Jesus was (and still is) a Master soul who incarnated on Earth to help humans find the path to spiritual enlightenment. As such, he remembered who he was and where he had come from and he knew his mission on Earth. His ability to focus his thoughts to manipulate matter and events allowed him to perform his miracles to attract attention to himself, so his message of love, forgiveness, and compassion could be heard by the masses.

"All thoughts are beams of energy that fan out from the thinker and affect matter and energy in the universe. The thoughts of most humans are weak and scattered, but focused thoughts can be very potent, just as the light from a laser is more powerful than the beam from a flashlight.

"Jesus and the other Masters who walked the Earth were adept at using focused thoughts to achieve 'wondrous and miraculous' results when needed to help others or to make a point. And Earth has been home to many Masters over the course of its history, like Moses,

Buddha, Mohammad, and others who have kept a low profile. Jesus and the other Masters were not gods or deities as has been claimed by religious holy men—rather they were very advanced souls who had risen to a level where they no longer needed to incarnate on Earth in order to grow and evolve. They all came to Earth to help other humans become more spiritually enlightened.

"The 'miracles' they performed while on Earth are things all souls can easily do on the Spirit Side by using 'thought creation.' In the Spirit Realm, all souls can walk on water or turn water into wine if they so desire. But when a soul incarnates on Earth, this ability to manipulate energy and matter is not available because most humans are not able to focus their thoughts to the degree necessary to accomplish such feats. All humans have the inherent ability to create 'miracles,' but they do not utilize enough of their brain power to get those results. Although some humans, like Masters, have developed this ability, most of them have not achieved this level of development. And so humans must plod along on the planet without the benefit of a 'magic wand' to make their hardships disappear and their triumphs flourish.

"All this, of course, flies in the face of what religious holy men have been preaching for centuries. They have told us that if we want something special, like passing a final exam, finding a good job, or being cured of a terminal illness, we need to pray to God for help. And if God deemed you worthy, He could make your wish come true. The reality, as stated before, is that God (or the Source) does not manipulate things or events on Earth and praying to God will not get you what you want.

"All thoughts, even unfocused thoughts, are beams of energy, and we can help ourselves by learning to focus our thoughts in meditation or otherwise, and the more focused your thoughts, the greater the chance your thoughts will be able to affect matter and energy to further your cause. And groups of people who all focus on the same thing have a more powerful effect on the world than the thoughts of one human. This is why group meditation can achieve much more than the thoughts (prayers) of any one individual."

"Because there will be no judgment or punishment for souls after they finish their lives on Earth, please tell us, Albert, how Hell fits into the cycle of reincarnation," Sophia chimed in when Albert stopped to catch his breath.

# ❦ Chapter Nine ❦
## *Hell No!*

Albert nodded his concurrence and continued:

"Many people on Earth live their lives in fear of what will happen to them when they die. They wonder if they will go to a wonderful place called Heaven or be sent to Hell as punishment for their sins. As mentioned before, Hell does not exist, and no one should be fearful of this outcome.

"This answer may surprise a lot of humans, especially those who were raised as Christians. Historically, the Church preached that Hell was an awful place where souls would burn in fires forever. The Church warned people that if they had committed a mortal sin and died before they made amends, they would be judged by God and He would send them to Hell for all eternity—a very scary thought, indeed.

"But the reality is that Hell does not exist—it was a fiction invented by religious holy men to control the masses through fear. As stated before, this fiction has been very effective over the ages in ensuring church pews were filled every Sunday, because few people would dare take the risk of ending up in the eternal fires of Hell.

"What really happens is very much different. When your physical bodies die, you will return to the Spirit Side, which is your true Home—the place you came from before you incarnated as humans. There is no judgment or punishment after you die, no matter what you did during your lives.

"You will incarnate as humans to learn lessons and face the challenges you need for your growth and evolution as souls, and all lives, even the bad ones, provide you with lessons that will enhance your knowledge and wisdom.

"So, have no fear about what will happen to you after you pass from your life on Earth, because you will always return to the peace and happiness of the Spirit Side no matter how often you went off course. And once back Home, you will be reunited with all your loved ones who passed before you."

At this point, a soul in the front row stood up and spoke: "If Hell does not exist, why do some people visit 'hell' during an NDE?"

Albert seemed to have expected this question, as he replied: "Near death experiences or NDEs have been reported often in the course of human history, especially so in recent times. NDEs usually happen to someone who has been clinically dead for a brief time before they are brought back to life. During this period of clinical death, the person's soul will leave the body and travel on the astral plane.

"Quite often, they will enter a place filled with love, light, and happiness where they will encounter loved ones who have already passed over. Sometimes they will find themselves in the presence of a religious figure like Jesus, Muhammad, Moses, Buddha, or God. In most cases, the person will be overwhelmed by the unconditional love and happiness of this place, and most will feel a strong desire to stay there and not return to their physical bodies on Earth.

"But despite their desire to stay, the person is told their time has not yet come, and they should return to Earth to complete their unfinished business. Reluctantly, they agree to return to their bodies, and, when they wake up back on Earth, they remember what they had experienced on their astral trip. For many, the trip to 'Heaven' marks a major turning point in the person's life, and they live the rest of their journey on the planet with a renewed understanding of who they are and their mission on Earth, comforted by the memories of the blissful place they will return to when their physical bodies die.

"Sometimes, in a small minority of cases, the person travels to a hellish place full of hideous, evil entities who terrify the poor soul and chase it back to its earthly body to escape. But if Hell does not exist, as I have mentioned frequently, what is this place that so closely resembles Hell?

"The answer is people who have NDEs are shown what their guides believe to be the best experience for them in order to send them on a new path of understanding and enlightenment. Unfortunately for some people, their guides feel they must create an illusion of Hell for them to encounter, because this is the best way to achieve a desired change in the person's life. But the hellish place they visit does not really exist—it is just an illusion created specially for them during their NDE.

"Rest assured Hell does not exist, and everyone gets to enjoy the love and happiness of the Spirit Side when they die, notwithstanding the tales of anguish and horror experienced by some people during an NDE."

"Thank you, Albert, for providing this assurance to the good souls who are here today," Sophia declared. "But many of the souls in the stands will no doubt wonder about the evil they will encounter in their new lives. I will do my best to explain why there is evil on Earth."

# ∿ Chapter Ten ∿
## *Evil on Earth*

"Earth is part of the universe that exists in the realm of lower vibrations and denser matter," Sophia explained. "It has a diverse climate, and some areas are extremely harsh for its inhabitants. Humans need oxygen, food, water, and shelter in order to survive, and the absence of any of these can cause discomfort, pain, or death. Earth does not have enough food or clean drinking water for everyone, and this often leads to strife among humans when those who do not have enough try to forcibly take what they need from other people.

"Earth is a school that provides incarnated souls the opportunity to experience things that do not exist on the Spirit Side. Souls on the Spirit Side do not have to eat, drink, breathe, find shelter, or accumulate wealth or material goods, and there is no suffering, sickness, or pain. Anything a soul wants on the Spirit Side can be created instantly through thought creation—a special process available on the Spirit Side that allows souls to create things instantly with the power of thought. As a result, there are no shortages of anything on the Spirit Side and no negative emotions. You cannot find anger, envy, or fear on the Spirit Side—only love and happiness.

"Earth is a place where souls can incarnate to encounter the harsh physical conditions that exist on this planet, the difficulties that result from these conditions, as well as the negative emotions of humans in response to these factors. The physical hardships arise from the vulnerability of human bodies to injury and disease and the interaction of humans with their physical environment. The negative emotions that people often generate flow from their reactions to these harsh conditions and their interactions with other humans. People feel discomfort or pain if they are hungry or thirsty, or if they are suffering from a disease or injury to their bodies. Fear and anxiety arise when they worry about having enough food and shelter for their families and being able to avoid injury and disease. Envy and jealousy result when people notice others have more material goods than they do, which also leads to anger and hate. These negative emotions frequently result in humans doing harmful things to other humans.

"Just as a survival school is designed to plunge its students into difficult conditions to teach them how to survive and come out alive, Earth is as a place for souls to feel its harsh physical conditions and the negative emotions that result from both a giving and receiving perspective.

"One of the main challenges for souls on Earth is to learn how to control the negative emotions they feel in response to the events that occur every day, including the actions of other people who are struggling to control their own negative emotions. People often inflict harm on others as a negative reaction to injury or disease to their bodies, to their harsh physical conditions, or in response to the actions or emotions of others.

"As souls live through all the facets of life in different incarnations, they continue to learn, gain wisdom, and evolve. Most souls require many lives before they reach a stage where they no longer need to incarnate on Earth in order to evolve to the next level.

"It is difficult for people to understand that all souls are making progress, albeit at different rates. The state of human affairs has changed greatly since they first arrived on Earth. In the early years, primitive men reacted in a very base way to the events around them. They lived in a savage society that was, to quote Thomas Hobbes, "… nasty, brutish, and short." It was typical then for people to become angry with those who stole their food, and this often ended in physical altercations.

"In most cases, souls do not plan to do evil deeds in their Life Plans; however, they know this may happen when they respond to the physical and emotional events they will face in their lives. Souls will often include challenging situations or temptations in their Life Plans as a test. They hope they will be able to control their emotions and resist harmful acts, but they know they may fail. A soul will include challenges in its Life Plan that are appropriate for it, taking into account its level of confidence and its stage of advancement. If a soul has failed these tests in past lives, it will likely include the temptations in subsequent Life Plans so it can get it right and move on to other things.

"Sometimes a soul will include harmful actions in its Life Plan at the request of another soul in order to help that other soul encounter the things it needs in its next life. For example, if a soul wants to know what it will be like to be abandoned by a parent during childhood, that soul might ask another soul in its spirit group to incarnate as its parent in order to fulfill this desire. In this case, the soul who agreed to be the parent will deliberately include this act of abandonment in its Life Plan.

"So, where does Satan figure into this picture? Many religions believe the devil is the prime instigator of evil, but the truth is Satan does not exist. He was created by religious leaders to be the focal point of all evil, an entity to be feared and vilified. It helped them explain why some very horrible events happened to their followers—

they could blame it on the devil. Religions often use the devil as a device to control their members. Their holy men preach that a person must be good and follow the rules of the religion, or the devil will take him away to Hell for all eternity. It is to their advantage to keep their congregations fearful of the devil since this will foster frequent attendance at church for protection and salvation.

"Like Hell, the devil does not exist. He is nothing more than a fictitious character invented by religious leaders to control the masses through fear. And there are no other demonic spirits who wreak havoc on unsuspecting humans, because all souls, when not physically embodied in the denser planes, are beings of pure energy who are intimately connected to the Source and to everyone else in the universe. And as the Source is love in its highest form, there is no room for anything on the Spirit Side other than wholesome, unfettered love.

"Unlike the Earth, evil does not exist in the Spirit Realm, and such term could never be applied to a soul over here no matter what it has done in its previous incarnations. The evil perpetrated by humans on Earth stays behind when their souls cross over to the Spirit Side, and the only baggage they bring back are the memories of their journeys on Earth.

"All souls are unique because they have all enjoyed different journeys since they spun out from the Source.

As a result, all souls have distinctive personalities that have evolved over the course of their incarnations on the denser planes. And this diversity is what makes the Spirit Side so special, as we can celebrate the sui generis nature of all souls as individual aspects of the Source.

"If a soul had been quiet and somber during its lives on Earth, it will likely project a similar personality in the Spirit Realm. And a soul who had lived its lives on Earth with gusto and exuberance will likely be the life of the party on this side of the veil. By the same token, those souls who loved pulling off pranks and other mischief as humans will often continue this behavior after they cross over.

"These mischievous spirits take delight in slamming doors, turning lights off and on, and levitating furniture, to startle and unnerve those people who frighten easily. These spirits are not evil, and they don't intend to cause any harm—they just enjoy a good laugh at the expense of superstitious humans. Unfortunately, some of their victims will believe they have encountered evil spirits, and they may suffer from nightmares as a result. There is no permanent harm done, despite the temporal discomfort felt by the timid.

"In a few cases, this type of paranormal activity is arranged by a soul in its prebirth planning as something needed for its evolution, and it recruits other souls to carry out these ghostly undertakings at the appropriate time.

"On occasion, these preternatural incidents result from the psychokinetic abilities of certain humans who can move objects with the power of thought. Sometimes these humans use their powers consciously to achieve a desired result, but often this power is deployed subconsciously by people who are frightened or under a great deal of stress.

"So, evil on the planet is not perpetrated by demons or evil spirits, because such entities do not exist. Evil on Earth is caused by humans who let their malevolent emotions rule their lives despite the best efforts of their souls and guides to steer them toward love and compassion. While there are evil humans who dish out a lot of violence on the planet, their souls are not evil in any sense, and those toxic emotions do not continue in the Spirit Realm."

"What about all the stories we have heard about people being possessed by evil spirits and needing an exorcism to cast the demons out of their bodies?" a curious soul from the audience wondered.

"I think you have watched too many reruns of the *Exorcist*," Sophia patiently explained. "And you are confusing the contrived horror created by Hollywood with reality. Like I said, there are no evil spirits, so it is not possible for them to invade a person's body, although I can understand why you would believe it to be possible.

"There is no doubt evil things happen on Earth,

but they are not caused by the devil or evil spirits. As I mentioned earlier, humans can suffer discomfort and pain from disease or injury to their bodies and from interacting with the physical conditions on this planet (such as volcanoes, hurricanes, earthquakes, and wildfires), which often leads to negative emotions and harmful actions. These factors are the natural consequences of humans living on planet Earth. The frailty of the human body and the physical conditions of this world are not inherently evil; they are what they are because of the natural evolution of humans and the physical attributes of the planet.

"People do not have to react negatively to the events around them, but all too often throughout the history of humankind this has been the result. Human response to negative events is not uniform; some people have learned to control their emotions and seldom cause any harm while others seem to have very little control over their emotions, and they often inflict physical or emotional pain on other humans.

"Earth is as a place for souls to face the varied challenges it has to offer, which are not available on the Spirit Side. These challenges provide souls the opportunity to learn and gain wisdom, so they can grow and evolve. Souls are fully aware of the conditions on Earth before they decide to incarnate, so there are no surprises for them.

"Have you ever heard someone on Earth say, 'there

is no frigging way I am coming back to this Hellhole'? I have heard that numerous times from people living on Earth, and you may well say that to yourself when everything seems to have fallen off the rails. What they mean, of course, is they don't want to return to Earth for another life. This is an understandable sentiment, given that life on Earth is full of difficult and painful challenges.

"This leads to the obvious question: Do you have a choice about reincarnating on Earth, or can you be forced to do so by the Source or the wheel of karma?

"As we pointed out before, the most important aspect to the cycle of reincarnation is that every soul has the right, at the end of each life, to choose where it goes next, without anyone interfering with this decision. Souls can freely choose to stay on the Spirit Side and relax, or they can decide to incarnate on Earth again or into another life form on a different planet. If they choose to incarnate again on Earth, they are free to develop a Life Plan that will provide them the challenges and lessons they need to further their evolution as souls. Souls can always get advice from the Council of Wise Ones on the best Life Plan for them, but they are free to accept or reject this advice.

"So now you might ask: 'If I have the right to never return to planet Earth, why in heaven's name would I choose to go back there?' From a human perspective, a vow to never return to Earth makes good sense. But when you return to the Spirit Side at the end of your life, you will be looking at things from a much different perspective.

"Once you have transitioned back to the Spirit Realm, you will regain all your memories of your previous lives and the goals for evolution you had established for yourselves in your Life Plans. From this perspective, you will be able to assess the progress you have made so far in your soul's evolution. If you feel another life on Earth is required to allow you to eventually graduate from the Earth school, then you will cheerfully, and with great determination, plan your next life on Earth, despite your previous vow to never return.

"Souls on the Spirit Side view a life on Earth as a very brief adventure on the denser planes. Because linear time, with a past, present, and future, does not exist in the Spirit Realm, a lifetime of eighty Earth years is merely like the blink of an eye on the Spirit Side. And because souls know they will always return to the blissful happiness of their Home no matter what they do on Earth, it is an easy decision to return to Earth for yet another life.

"You can never be trapped on the wheel of karma, unless you choose to do so. If you have cumulative negative karma from your lives on Earth, you are not compelled to return until you have paid your karmic debt, but most souls will voluntarily choose to do so as a moral imperative—a desire to continue with lives on Earth until the scales are balanced.

"When you are having your journey on Earth, you can vow over and over until you are blue in the face that you will never return to this planet, but the reality is that you may very well change your mind once you are back on the Spirit Side. This prospect should give you something to chew on as you plan your earthly trek.

"Unless there are any questions, I will turn it over to Albert once more so he can tell you about Gaia, the consciousness of planet Earth."

# Chapter Eleven
## Gaia Speaks

Albert pointed to a holographic projection of Earth, and responded:

"As Sophia mentioned, Gaia is the consciousness of planet Earth. I have had several conversations with Gaia about what is happening to Mother Earth, and I found her to be a wise and compassionate entity who is very protective of the planet and all its flora and fauna.

"She told me the planet is under siege and the effects of climate change are very noticeable: greater fluctuations in temperature, as well as more frequent natural disasters with ever-increasing intensity, such as floods, hurricanes, typhoons, tornadoes, droughts, wildfires, and earthquakes. And much of the blame for this can be laid at the feet of humans.

"Gaia has watched all the developments on Earth from the very creation of the planet until the present day, and so she has a unique perspective on all the changes that have happened over the aeons. Gaia's goal has always been to maintain a balanced ecological system in which all plants and animals can flourish without any major disruptions. Many of the notable disasters in Earth's history, like the extinction of most of the dinosaurs sixty-five million years ago, resulted from cosmological events that were beyond the control of Gaia. (She was powerless to stop the asteroid from striking the Yucatan Peninsula.)

"But many of the things that contribute to climate change are caused directly or indirectly by humans on the planet. In the early days of human civilization when they lived relatively primitive lives, they did not make a large environmental footprint on the planet. The industrial revolution changed things in a drastic fashion, as the pollution caused by humans began to have a significant effect on Mother Earth, and this trend has continued to the present day at a frenetic pace.

"Humans have caused significant disruptions to the delicate ecosystems of the planet by dumping toxic waste and plastic into the rivers and oceans, poisoning the soil with chemicals, and fouling the air with noxious fumes. Humans continue to spew toxins into the atmosphere in ever-increasing amounts, and the sprawl of their towns and cities into nearby farms and forests, and destruction of huge swaths of rain forest, has curbed Mother Earth's ability to absorb the extra carbon dioxide.

"Humans not only abuse the planet with their pollution, but their reckless disregard for the consequences of their actions also imperils the well-being of the other creatures on the planet who are powerless to stop the abuse.

"Gaia is extremely upset about the abuse humans heap on Mother Earth and her other creatures every day. She is fiercely protective of all her flora and fauna, including humans, but is increasingly skeptical humans will be able to change their ways before it is too late. She views humankind as a toxic weed that invades the garden, snuffing out all other life in its path. And humans also directly abuse the other creatures by hunting and killing them for sport or food, imprisoning them in zoos and water parks, entangling them in nets and traps, and shrinking their natural habitant with urban and agricultural sprawl.

"Gaia does not understand how humans continue to foul their home planet with their pollution and abuse. She wonders why humans have not realized it is not prudent to 'crap' on their own doorstep. Gaia knows that some humans understand the problem and are trying to make positive changes, but humankind as a whole still has a long way to go to alleviate the problem. Too many people do not understand the depth of the problem or just do not care. She believes it is important for those who are enlightened to educate the masses and their governments and persuade them to take the necessary action to curb and eliminate their pollution before all life on Earth is destroyed.

"Gaia told me she has the ability to manipulate the weather and geological conditions on the planet, and in recent times she has increased the number and intensity of natural disasters around the world as a 'wake-up call' for humans—a warning shot across their bow. She loves humans as much as her other creatures and does not wish to wipe us off the face of the planet, but she will do her best to make us realize we must change our ways or suffer the consequences."

At this point Albert placed a large black loudspeaker on the stage and pressed a few buttons. Soon a smooth, melodious voice came through: "Greetings, Albert. How can I help you today?"

"I am teaching an orientation class with Sophia, and I hoped you could fill them in on what is happening in your corner of the cosmos," Albert announced.

"With pleasure, Albert," Gaia responded. "Over the past while I have been working hard to raise my vibrations so I can ascend to a higher dimension, but humans are holding me back. All my other creatures are ready to make the transition. However, it cannot move forward as long as humans are stuck in the morass of slow vibrations and dense matter. Some humans have made the transition, although most humans still do not understand what must be done to make the ascension. The deterrent for humans is their inability to curb their pernicious emotions, like fear, anger, hate, and greed, which is the cause of all the conflicts and wars that occur on a regular basis. If they would only embrace love and forgiveness for all, they would expand their consciousness and increase their vibrations to allow everyone to ascend to a higher dimension.

"Many of my creatures, like dolphins, whales, elephants, and chimpanzees, to name a few, are highly intelligent, sentient beings who understand where we need to go and are dismayed at how humans seem oblivious to the urgent need for them to get their act together before they crash and burn. The negativity of humans casts a dark pall over Mother Earth—a stifling shroud that unjustly impedes our ascension to a higher dimension where there is nothing but love, peace, and harmony.

"When humans were first seeded on Mother Earth aeons ago, I had high hopes they would evolve into intelligent, benevolent, and peace-loving beings who would be admired by all my other creatures as paragons of virtue. Somewhere along the way they took a wrong turn, and the rest of us have had to endure the appalling consequences ever since.

"I speak to humans every day through the sounds of nature: the rustle of leaves in the breeze, the babbling of a brook in the forest, and the crashing of the surf on a rocky beach, except most humans do not hear my message because they are too busy chasing money and power. This is why I have enlisted you, and all my other messengers, to spread the word to all who will listen.

"I wish all humans could have the opportunity to converse with me, and then no doubt I believe things would quickly change for the better. Unfortunately, this is unlikely to happen any time soon, so those humans who understand the problem must work harder to persuade all other humans to take up the cause," Gaia concluded.

This exchange reminded me that I have had the privilege (during my astral trips with Albert) of seeing our planet from space and admiring its breathtaking beauty. It is like a jeweled pendant hanging in the inky blackness of space—a sight to behold and cherish. It would be a shame if this exquisite orb were to become a toxic, barren wasteland, devoid of all life. We all must pitch in to save this place we call home.

Does this mean our planet is doomed? One need only watch the evening news or read a newspaper to become apprehensive about the prospects for our civilization and the planet we inhabit. We have developed technology that makes our lives easier and more comfortable than was the case a century ago, but we have not progressed very much with our ability to deal with the toxic emotions that have plagued humankind from the beginning of time.

Humans today still allow fear, anger, hate, and jealousy to control too much of our lives, resulting in wars, genocide, murder, mass shootings, terrorist acts, and other violent conflicts. Our emotional and spiritual intelligence has not kept pace with our scientific achievements, and the result is that we have greatly improved our ability to kill one another without a corresponding recognition that we must embrace love and not let fear dominate our lives.

Albert and Sophia have noted that some of the earlier advanced civilizations on Earth, like Atlantis and Lemuria, rose to great heights before they collapsed. They had developed breakthrough technology that provided their citizens with a comfortable way of life, but they failed to rein in their toxic emotions, and their technology ultimately became the driving force behind their tragic downfall. Humans today must be mindful of these lessons, otherwise they are doomed to repeat their mistakes.

According to Albert and Sophia, the solution for our civilization is simple in concept, but difficult to implement. In order to avoid a catastrophic disaster, we must learn to stifle our negative emotions and fully embrace love and compassion for ourselves, all other humans, and Mother Earth herself. Once we understand we are all souls having a human journey on Earth, and we are intimately connected to the Source and to each other, it will be much easier for us to love others and forgive them for their past transgressions. When love becomes the dominant emotion, we won't have any need for wars or weapons of mass destruction, and we will finally be able to live in peace and harmony with our fellow humans, as well as Mother Earth and the other creatures who share our planet.

To get there will take a concerted effort by every one of us. We must take one step at a time, beginning with ourselves. When we learn to live with love, our negative emotions will melt away like a snowbank in the spring, and we will become shining examples for everyone we encounter. The goodness we generate will fan out to induce others to follow our lead, and gradually our civilization will pull out of the depths of despair to enter a new paradigm of peace and harmony.

We must hasten our efforts to achieve this state of grace before the negative forces that lurk in our world cause an irreversible calamity to consume us all. Can we pull this off? Albert tells me he is optimistic our civilization will survive and thrive, but we must be vigilant and determined in our march toward love and respect for one another. Failure to do so could be disastrous for our beautiful planet.

Albert and Sophia bade farewell to Gaia, and announced that the orientation class would resume later, giving all the souls in the stadium a chance to digest what they have learned so far.

I followed Albert back to Earth and slipped into my physical body, hoping Albert would return to get me when the orientation class resumed.

# ᨆ Chapter Twelve ᨆ
## *Pandemic*

I am writing this chapter is the middle of the coronavirus pandemic that is raging around our planet.

When Albert returned to my bedroom the next night (in the spring of 2020) to take me back to the orientation class, I asked him if we could first make a side trip to visit Gaia, so I could ask her about the coronavirus pandemic that had been plaguing our planet. Like most people in the world, we were under lockdown restrictions that required us to stay at home and go out only for essentials, like groceries and medicine. And I hoped Gaia could shed some light on the pandemic.

So, off we went to the same cavern under the North Pole where I had first encountered Gaia.

"Hello, Gaia," I called out tentatively. "Do you have time for a few questions?"

"Of course, Garnet, I always have time for you. And I want to thank you for including my previous messages to humankind in your books. Hopefully, my entreaties to your fellow humans will be taken seriously so the abuse your civilization has heaped on Mother Earth and her other creatures will decline and eventually cease altogether."

"I want to ask you about the coronavirus pandemic that is ravaging our world. What can you tell me about this plague?" I ventured.

"This pandemic is part of the periodic cleansing Mother Earth instigates from time to time. Right now, your planet is trying to guide humans toward a new paradigm, a new world order, which will curb the pollution of your planet and stop the abuse they heap on one another and the other creatures who share the planet.

"As you know, your human civilization is non-egalitarian and elitist, with only a few people controlling most of the wealth, while the people at the bottom end of the economic ladder live in poverty. The rich countries in the world hoard money and resources, leaving many humans without enough food, clean water, or medicine.

"The pandemic is a wake-up call for humans—another shot across their bow. Although I love humans as much as the other creatures on your planet, it is humans who have become the driving force behind the degradation of the ecosystem on planet Earth. Humanity is like an invasive weed that is taking over the garden, snuffing out all other life in its path. This is due to the unbridled arrogance of the human race that believes they are the only occupants of the planet that have relevance and importance, and the other creatures are merely expendable vassals who must give way to the needs and desires of homo sapiens.

"Not only do humans abuse other animals without justification, they cause great harm to Mother Earth with their pollution. They dump their garbage into the rivers, lakes, and oceans, poison the soil with toxic chemicals, and spew noxious fumes into the atmosphere. This causes great harm to Mother Earth and her other beloved creatures, and it must stop.

"Mother Earth has unleashed pandemics in the past, such as the Black Death of the fourteenth century (75–200 million deaths), and the Spanish flu of 1918 (50 million deaths). And history shows that past pandemics have reshaped societies in profound ways. Millions of people have perished, empires have fallen, governments have been overthrown, and entire generations have been decimated.

"The coronavirus pandemic will eventually end, but only after thousands and thousands of people have died. The isolation lockdown in most countries will be a great time for humans to reflect on their role in the future of your civilization and the well-being of planet Earth. I implore humans to take these events seriously before it is too late."

"Thank you, Gaia, for your insights on this dreadful

pandemic. I will relay your message in my next book, but I hope the current pandemic will have passed by the time it is published. Nevertheless, your dictum is something we should all keep in mind as we go forward, with the hope Mother Earth will not need to unleash any more cleansing pandemics."

Albert and I bade farewell to Gaia and floated out of the cavern to return to the Spirit Side and the orientation class in the amphitheater.

Before we reached the amphitheater I asked Albert a question that had been on my mind for several days: "Before my first incarnation on Earth, did I attend an orientation class as a newbie to the Earth plane?"

"You did indeed," Albert replied. "But you were not a good student. You kept on falling asleep during the lectures, and your loud snoring was disruptive to the class. And what was worse, after the orientation was finished, you announced you were not going to incarnate on Earth because it was too tough of a school, and many of the other souls decided to follow your lead. We did not want this to happen, as Earth was in desperate need of souls who could cast aside the darkness with their beacons of light.

"We finally had to resort to a bribe to get you to change your mind: We promised you could eat all the perogies and cabbage rolls you wanted in your new life.

This worked very well and, judging by your bulging waistline, you managed to eat your way through this life as well."

"Very funny, Albert. You told me once humor was alive and well on the Spirit Side, but for some reason you missed out when they were handing out the humor pills."

"You can't hide anything from me, Garnet, so don't pretend. I was watching you when you stepped on the talking scale the other day and it told you 'one at a time, please.'"

I threw up my hands in exasperation, as I had learned once again Albert will always have the last word. When we reached the amphitheater, I took my seat in the front row and listened as Sophia continued her discourse.

# ᘐᖇ Chapter Thirteen ᖇᘐ
## *New Earth*

"Much has been said in recent years about the New Earth, also known to some people as 5d Earth," Sophia explained. "The cognoscenti has proclaimed that humans live in 3d Earth, and their destiny is to ascend to Earth in a higher dimension where there are no wars, conflicts, violence, crime, or toxic emotions. In this utopia everyone lives in peace and harmony with one another, with the other creatures who share the planet, and with Mother Earth herself.

"The New Earth is like the Old Earth in terms of climate, vegetation, and geography, but it is different in very important ways. It exists concurrently with the Old Earth, but it has a higher vibration rate as it spins around the sun in a higher, parallel dimension. The New Earth is populated with plants, animals, and humans, much like the Old Earth, except there are some major differences that make the New Earth seem like paradise when compared to the Old Earth.

"Humans on the New Earth are peace-loving people

who are not plagued with negative emotions. As such, they live in peace and harmony with each other without any crime, violence, or aggressive behavior. There is no money or accumulation of material goods, and no one must work for a living. Everything a person needs to live a happy and comfortable life, including food, shelter, clothing, and entertainment, is provided free of charge by their society. Everyone is on equal footing, so there is no competition or jealousy among its citizens. They have ample opportunity to enjoy themselves in sporting and recreational activities, and they can learn about their planet and the universe in the classrooms, libraries, and knowledge archives on their planet. If they are so inclined, they can pursue a career in all the different fields to help make their planet an even better place to live. Or, they can choose to simply enjoy life in this idyllic society.

"The citizens of the New Earth honor and respect Mother Earth, so they do not pollute their planet in any way. They pride themselves on having a zero-emissions environmental footprint, as they know it is foolish to foul the planet they call home. They also treat the animals with dignity and respect, and they do not consume animal flesh or otherwise kill, injure, or imprison the fauna of their planet.

"The humans on this planet have eradicated all the diseases that plague the Old Earth, they have learned how to repair accidental injury to their bodies, and they know how to slow down the aging process. As a result, its citizens live for several hundred years, and they usually transition to the Spirit Side only when they feel it is time to move on and continue their evolution in a different environment.

"The New Earth is not a future event. The planet Earth exists simultaneously in several different dimensions, each with different vibratory rates. The Old Earth is on the lowest step of the ladder—the dimension with the lowest vibratory rate and densest matter—while the New Earth is further up the ladder in a dimension with a higher vibratory rate. But the New Earth is not something that will happen in the future—it has always existed simultaneously with the Old Earth.

"Humans living on the Old Earth have vibration rates that match the vibration frequencies of their planet. If they want to transition to the New Earth, they must increase their vibratory rates to match vibrations of that planet. Some humans have already done this and many more are working toward this goal. Not everyone living today on the Old Earth, however, will make the transition in their current lifetimes, but their souls will return to the Spirit Side when their physical bodies die because no one is ever left behind. Once they are back on the Spirit Side, they can decide if they want to reincarnate into a human on the Old Earth to help the remaining humans make the shift, or they can choose to incarnate into a human who has already made the transition to the New Earth."

"Is the New Earth the same as the Spirit Side?" a soul at the back of the amphitheater piped up.

"No, it is not the same. The New Earth still exists on the physical plane, only it is not as dense as the Old Earth as a result of its higher vibratory rate. Humans on the New Earth still have physical bodies, although they have shed all their negative emotions and live in a world of love, peace, and harmony. And because they have learned how to focus their thoughts into powerful beams of energy, they are able to easily manipulate matter and manifest whatever they desire. There are no shortages of material goods on the New Earth and no need for humans to fight each other for the things they all want.

"Humans in the New Earth often live for several hundred years, because they can control the aging process, resist disease, and heal bodily injuries. Their physical bodies die when their souls decide it is time to return to the Spirit Side, not as a result of old age or disease.

"On the other hand, souls on the Spirit Side do not have physical bodies; they are like beings of pure energy. While the New Earth has some of the positive characteristics of the Spirit Side, it is not the same. The New Earth is partway up the vibratory ladder, while the

Spirit Side is at the very top."

"What will become of the Old Earth when all humans have made the transition?" the same soul asked.

"The Old Earth will continue to exist simultaneously with the New Earth. When all humans have made the shift, it will go through a natural cleansing process to rid itself of all the garbage and pollution left behind by humans. Once this has been completed, it will be able to make the shift to a higher dimension and merge with the New Earth.

"What happens if the remaining humans do not make the transition because they have destroyed all life on the Old Earth with their pollution or weapons of mass destruction?" yet another soul in the stands wondered.

"In that case, the souls of those killed in the destruction will return to the Spirit Side, except they will not have the option of incarnating again on the Old Earth. If this happens, Old Earth will have to go through a much longer cleansing process before it is ready for new life forms and the shift to a higher dimension. In the worst-case scenario, it will remain as a barren and lifeless planet with no further prospects for harboring life.

"The New Earth is like a paradise compared to the Old Earth, so how do humans get there? The answer is simple, but the implementation is difficult. The New Earth has a much higher vibration rate than the Old Earth and the people who reside there. To ascend to utopia, humans must raise their vibrations to match those of the New Earth. When this happens, a person will pop up to the higher dimension like a cork being released from beneath the surface of the water.

"And how do humans raise their vibrations? They must stifle their toxic emotions and fully embrace love, compassion, and forgiveness. This means they must stop judging others for what they have done in the past, and stop being fearful of people who have a different color of skin, speak a different language, have different customs, or worship a different God. They must control their urge to lash out at someone who has stepped on their toes and stop comparing themselves to others, which causes jealousy and unhappiness.

"It is important for all humans to acknowledge that all other people are souls, just like them, who are having a human incarnation on the planet without the benefit of knowing who they are or where they came from. And when they realize all souls are intimately connected to the Source and to each other, the tendency to embrace all others with love will flow naturally like water cascading down a mountain stream.

"This may seem like a formidable task; however, you can take comfort that many humans from the Old Earth have made the physical ascension to the New Earth over the history of humankind, mostly as individuals, but sometimes as groups of like-minded people."

As I listened to Sophia, I recalled one of my trips to the Spirit Side with Albert where I encountered a soul who had incarnated on the Old Earth and eventually made the ascension to the New Earth. She had been living a happy life as a young woman with a husband and two young children. But then her world was torn asunder when a drunk driver ran a red light and T-boned her husband's vehicle, killing him and her two children. After spiraling down into the depths of despair, she was persuaded to attend an ashram in India where she learned to meditate. When she was finally able to forgive the man who killed her family and forgive God for allowing this to happen, she awoke one day from a deep meditation to find herself in a different place: she had ascended to the New Earth.

If she can do it, so can we all. And you don't have to experience a tragic event to spur you on—you just need to remember to fully embrace love and incorporate this into your everyday life. Bon voyage!

I snapped out of my reverie as Sophia announced to the class that she had arranged for a special guest to speak to the class. And my excitement mounted as I watched Jesus take center stage to address the students.

# ᕦ Chapter Fourteen ᕤ
## *Son of God*

Sophia proudly introduced her guest: "Our guest speaker today is Jesus Christ, the inspiration for the Christian Church on Earth. Because this religion has so many followers and plays such an important role in world affairs, I think it would be useful for you to understand how this all came about so you may be better able to plan your upcoming incarnation on Earth.

"Dear Jesus, welcome to our class. Could you please tell us how it came to be that you engendered this religion so long ago?"

Jesus bowed graciously and began his tale: "Before I incarnated as the human known as Jesus, I had several planning discussions with the Council of Wise Ones. We all agreed humanity needed a spiritual uplifting to steer it toward an expanded consciousness that would promote love and forgiveness in lieu of fear, anger, and hate. As I was an advanced soul who was familiar with human incarnations on the Earth plane, the Council asked me to take on this assignment, and I accepted without hesitation.

"After my birth I was allowed to pierce through the veil of forgetfulness so I could remember where I came from and my mission in life. This helped me plan the steps I needed to implement my vocation, which was to lead my people out of the darkness. This is why I traveled to Tibet to study under the Buddhist monk known as Choden during the so-called lost years when the scriptures make no mention of my activities. In Tibet I learned how to meditate and to focus my thoughts into powerful beams of energy, so I could manipulate matter in magical ways.

"I knew my words alone would not be powerful enough to garner the attention of the masses once I began my public ministry, so I performed the 'miracles' described in the gospels to attract attention and encourage my followers to view me as a scion of God. I understood my teachings would have the greatest impact if I could persuade the people I spoke the word of God, pointing the way to everlasting salvation.

"That part worked well, and I was able to preach to my followers with an aura of divinity that convinced some of them I was the long-awaited Messiah. And my last miracle in that life—rising from the dead after my crucifixion—was the key factor that persuaded the early architects of the Church I was the son of God.

"This set the stage for the genesis of a new religion that could lead the people out of the darkness and into the light. The early leaders of the Church only needed to disseminate my teachings to the masses, and the truthfulness of my words would soon have become apparent to all.

"My core message was simple yet powerful: love your neighbor as you love yourself and treat others as you would like to be treated. If everyone followed these principles faithfully, there would be no violence or crime, no wars or genocide, and no discrimination based on language, customs, skin color, or sexual orientation. My teachings beseech all people to unconditionally love and forgive themselves and all their fellow humans.

"For the most part, I am pleased with the development of the Church in the wake of my death on the cross. They have been effective in promulgating my teachings to the masses, and this has provided guidance and hope for the people who were searching for meaning in their lives. The Church has sponsored good deeds throughout the world through their charities, and they have always encouraged their congregations to donate time and money to help the sick and needy members of society.

"I am especially proud of the foot soldiers of the Church—the priests, ministers, nuns, and brothers who have worked tirelessly over the years to spread my message of love and hope to those who had been floundering in the darkness, because their efforts have contributed a lot to the betterment of society. For all these good deeds of the Church, I am thankful, and I encourage all Christian clergy to keep up the good work.

"The bad news is that somehow along the way my message became marginalized to some degree by the leaders of the Church who were focused on increasing their membership rosters as a way to enhance their power and control over the masses. To that end, they embellished the story of my life on Earth to lure more people into the fold who could be cajoled to empty their pockets into the Church coffers.

"They decided I should be deified as the son of God, an equal member of the Holy Trinity that includes God the father and the Holy Spirit. And to prop up their assertion of my divinity, they decreed I was conceived by divine intervention when my mother was impregnated by the Holy Spirit. It was a wonderful story to sell to their credulous followers, and it glorified my image as the founding pillar of the Church who died on the cross to save them from their sins.

"And to ensure I was considered to be as pure as the driven snow, they proclaimed I never married and was celibate all my life, because, in their distorted view of humanity, people who are sullied by base and demeaning activities, like sexual intercourse, cannot be truly godlike and holy.

"The reality, of course, is that I was conceived in the normal fashion through the sexual union of my mother and father, and I was married to Mary Magdalene, who gave birth to our three children. But the holy men who fabricated these stories went to great pains to ensure all scriptures describing my life were edited to conform to their version of my life.

"The embellishment of my story has not caused any direct harm to anyone, except it was just the beginning of a series of misguided capers the leaders of the Church foisted on their unsuspecting followers over the years, some of which have caused a great deal of hardship and pain.

"Leading the pack was their cynical decision to control the masses through guilt and fear. They devised a myriad of rules for the faithful to follow, claiming they came from God. These rules governed not only a person's conduct in society but dictated all the steps necessary for the proper worship of the Lord. And they decreed that people breaking these rules would offend God and, if they did not make amends before they died, He would pass judgment on them as sinners and send them to Hell for all eternity. Controlling people through guilt and fear has been a very effective tool for the Church, but it has caused plenty of hardship along the way.

"You can't imagine all the mental anguish this has

caused people over the ages—all the sleepless nights suffered by those who were afraid they or someone they loved would end up in the painful fires of Hell without any hope for redemption. And people who live in fear tend to react to the events in their lives with anger and hate, which fuels a vicious cycle of violence and abuse.

"Although coercing people with the threat of eternal damnation filled the pews every Sunday, this tactic fosters fear rather than love. I do not need to be worshipped, and I do not expect people to attend a church service every week, or at all. I only wish humans would follow my teachings and love one another with joy in their hearts.

"And even worse than the mental anguish they have engendered, some of the overzealous fanatics of the Church have inflicted inexcusable pain and suffering on innocent people who had committed no crime other than worshipping a different god. I am referring to all the Muslims who were killed when their cities were sacked and pillaged by crusading Christians, and to the thousands of Jews who were tortured and killed during the Inquisitions.

"I am surprised and upset at all the violence Christians have instigated in my name over the years, especially when you consider I never advocated or encouraged violence for any reason when I lived on Earth. It still amazes me that some humans managed to use my legacy as the justification for their brutal acts of violence against people who belonged to a different religion.

"And although such barbarity has long since been relegated to the history books, the Catholic Church today still attempts to enforce misguided laws that are not derived from my teachings, including the prohibitions on divorce and artificial birth control and the celibacy policy for priests. These rules were not inspired by me, and they serve no useful purpose in society. I cringe when I think about all the unnecessary guilt and anguish they have generated over the years in the people who breached these laws for good reasons.

"I guess I never should have expected the Christian religion to unfold perfectly, because it has been guided by inherently imperfect men who had to struggle with all the challenges of a human journey on Earth.

"I sincerely hope that those of you who decide to incarnate on Earth will do your best to promote my teachings to your fellow humans in a spiritually enlightened manner. Good luck to you all."

Jesus waved at the crowd as he left the stage, and Sophia resumed her place on center stage.

"We are about to wrap up this class, and I hope we have given you a few valuable insights about incarnating on Earth. As you consider your options, feel free to discuss any issues you may have with me, Albert, or any member of the Council.

"Before we disperse, I will ask Albert to provide some parting words of wisdom."

# Chapter Fifteen
## *Words of Wisdom*

Albert nodded at Sophia, and addressed the class:

"There some important things to remember if you decide to take the plunge for a life on Earth.

"Every soul has chosen its own path for evolution, which is why all lives on Earth are unique. Humans should not pass judgment on the actions of others, because they do not know anything about the other person's previous incarnations or what that person had mapped out in their Life Plans. And you won't know what challenges that person is now facing or may already have experienced in their current lives.

"When you meet somebody on the street wearing unusual clothes, speaking a foreign language, or displaying a different color of skin, you must understand that even though their outward appearance is not the same as yours, they are souls just like you having a human journey on Earth. When you realize all souls are intimately connected to the Source and to one another, your love for others will flow as naturally as the love you have for your family.

Whatever joy or pain you bestow on others will be the joy or pain you inflict on yourself.

"And self-love is the starting point for all love on Earth. You cannot truly love others until you love yourself unconditionally. This means you must forgive yourself for all your past mistakes without harboring any guilt or remorse. And forgiving yourself makes it easier for you to forgive those people who have wronged you in the past.

"This reality was stated succinctly by Jesus when he said: 'Do to others as you would have them do to you,' because whatever you do to others you are actually doing to yourself. And since the other creatures who share the planet have souls as well, this also applies to animals. If you can keep this in mind as you go about your daily business, Earth will be a happier place for all its inhabitants.

"And you must appreciate that many humans do not yet see the light. They are mired in hurtful emotions and let their fear, anger, hate, and greed control too much of their lives. They need someone to shine a light on the path to spiritual enlightenment, which is why we implore you to be one of our torch bearers. We hope your journeys on Earth will be fruitful, and you will allow your light to penetrate the darkness for those people who still stumble about in the shadows.

"There is only one thought, one message to give to other humans: Love. All Masters who have walked the

Earth have revealed, in their own way, that love is the answer to all the problems on the planet. If you fully embrace unconditional love, fear, and all its derivatives, like hate, anger, and greed, will disappear like dew in the morning sunlight. If you love all other people you will have no need to judge them for who they are or what they have done in the past. And you will not fear those people who speak a different language, have a different skin color, or worship a different God.

"Humans must accept the differences among their people as unique deviations spawned by the limitless creativity of the Source. The Source could have created all humans as identical clones, but this would have eliminated many of the challenges that make the planet a difficult school, a place where souls can prove themselves worthy of continued evolution as scions of the Source.

"On the Spirit Side, unconditional love comes naturally without any special effort because that is all there is at this level of existence. Unfortunately, when souls pass through the veil of forgetfulness as part of the incarnation process, they do not remember where they came from, and they must struggle to recall who they really are and why they chose a human journey on Earth. This has always been the challenge for humans on the planet, and it will not change anytime soon.

"As Sophia has explained, humans are at a crucial

point in their development and it is incumbent on all people who have seen the light to spread the message of love and hope from Spirit. When you incarnate on Earth you must do your part, along with the other people who channel Spirit, to help others find their way on the path to spiritual awareness. And maybe someday, with the blessing of the Council, I will join you back on Earth in this important crusade.

"Once on Earth, you will have the same hang-ups that plague most souls having a human incarnation. You will be frustrated because you won't know for sure where you should be going, and you will be fearful of taking a wrong turn or making a mistake. Think of your life as a vast labyrinth of paths with numerous twists and turns, except there are no dead ends and you will always be able to find your way out of the maze. You will enjoy valuable life lessons no matter which path you choose, even when you stray off the path you had planned before you incarnated. Remember to relax and enjoy life wherever it may take you.

"Of course, you will encounter many difficulties and obstacles on your journey, which is all part and parcel of a human incarnation. It is important for you to learn to recognize the difference between an obstacle meant to be overcome and a brick wall at the end of a dead-end street. In the case of the former, it is usually designed to test your determination—to see if you can persevere in a difficult situation without giving up. When you come upon this kind of obstruction, you should dig down deep, push your way through, and savor the satisfaction that will flow from this victory.

"On the other hand, if you find yourself staring at a brick wall that is blocking your path there is nothing to be gained by crashing into the bricks in a senseless rage. If this happens, you need to back away gracefully and find another street to continue your journey. Brick walls are life's way of telling you that you need to change direction.

"The real challenge is learning to tell one from the other. My advice to you is to listen to your feelings and follow your heart. Your intuition is never wrong, but your mind often is. When facing obstacles, you must strive to rein in the thoughts that charge around your mind like wild horses on the loose and focus your attention on the whispers from your guides. Your guides are always there for you, and they will not let you down.

"Unfortunately, there is no magic sword I can give you to slay the fears and uncertainties that will often rear their ugly heads in your new life.

"You must remind yourself everyday about the nature of your journey and who you really are. Do not view your life too seriously and learn to lighten up and enjoy your sojourn on Earth. Try to see the humor in the world around you and laugh at your foibles and the antics of your fellow humans, just as we do in the Spirit Realm. Nothing that happens on Earth continues after death, and the only things you will take with you are the memories of your life and the wisdom you gleaned from your journey on Earth.

"Remember to reach out to touch the Source every day. Pause often to hug your spouse and children, cradle your grandchildren in your arms, and give your pets a few pats. Smile at strangers you pass on the street and be generous to the homeless people asking for handouts, because they are all souls who are connected to you and to each other as individual aspects of the Source. Let your actions display the compassion all humans should feel for each other and for the other creatures on your planet.

"Forgive those who step on your toes because, like you, they are still learning about the dance of life on Earth. Do not waste your energy comparing yourself to other people as you are all distinct aspects of the Source experiencing a human journey designed to fulfill your requirements for wisdom and growth. And since every soul has mapped out its own unique path for evolution, you should respect the life choices made by others with understanding and compassion. And never make judgments about other people because you do not know where they have been or where they are going.

"Respect all other creatures living on Earth as they too are individual aspects of the Source who incarnated on the planet to experience what it has to offer. Treat them with dignity and kindness and do your best to halt the abuse heaped on them by other humans. Lead by example whenever you encounter the critters that share your planet and be willing to step up to the plate whenever necessary to stop their suffering.

"Honor Mother Earth for all the gifts she will provide to you each and every day. Make sure you are not contributing to the pollution of this beautiful planet and speak out forcefully whenever possible to implore your fellow humans to stop abusing the environment.

"And remember to embrace all other humans with love and compassion and treat everyone the way you would like to be treated yourself. Discard your illusions of separation and acknowledge every day that you are all connected to each other and to the Source. Be part of the crusade to distribute the bounty harvested from Mother Earth to all people on the planet, regardless of where they live.

"You are an eternal spirit about to have a human journey in a life you will choose for yourself, and you will be the creator of your own reality. Choose hope instead of fear, love and not hate, and happiness over despair, and your time on Earth will be much more rewarding. Death should not be feared because it is merely a doorway leading you back Home to the warm embrace of your loved ones. Relax, enjoy your adventure, and relish all your life experiences, because you cannot become lost no matter which path you follow.

"And don't rush through life like you are running a sprint. You are on a journey that has no timetable and no finish line, so slow down and enjoy life to the fullest. Do not be afraid to break out of your comfort zone and try different things because failure is not an option, and you will grow and evolve from every new adventure. And do not be concerned about what other people think of you, because it is your journey to enjoy, not theirs."

Albert and Sophia bowed to the crowd and waved in response to the standing ovation. Soon the stands emptied as the eager souls scurried off to plan their next adventure on planet Earth.

Albert left the stage and joined me in the stands. I was curious as to what he had planned for me next, and I soon found out. He told me I was about to meet one of the smartest men to have lived in the twentieth century, and I eagerly followed him out of the amphitheater toward the main entrance portal of Aglaia.

# ꧁ Chapter Sixteen ꧂
## *Genius*

I walked with Albert along a stone path that meandered through the lush green meadow beside Aglaia. The wildflowers bordering the path seemed to be especially resplendent with a dazzling array of vibrant colors, and the perfume that wafted up from these blossoms was exhilarating.

When we reached a bench under a majestic sequoia tree, we sat down to enjoy the splendor of the garden. Before long, we noticed a short man with bushy hair ambling toward us. He settled into an Adirondack chair facing our bench and greeted us with a warm smile.

As soon as I realized this was Albert Einstein, one of the greatest minds of the twentieth century, my excitement was palpable. I had so many questions for him that I hardly knew where to begin. He seemed to sense my bewilderment, so he waited patiently for me to sort out my thoughts.

"It is a great honor to meet you, sir," I began at last. "May I ask you a few questions?"

"Of course. Fire away. I have all the time in the world," he responded with a wink.

"From your current perspective, what would you say was your greatest achievement during your life on Earth?"

"Most certainly, it was to encourage humans to think outside of the box and understand that our universe is much more complex than previously thought when our reality was based on Newtonian physics. Sir Isaac's theories captured the essence of our microcosm as we perceived it at the time, but it did not accurately describe the actions of energy and matter from a cosmic or subatomic perspective. Sir Isaac did an amazing job with his theories, considering the crude and elementary science he had to work with. I have the greatest respect for Sir Isaac, and we have had many congenial discussions over here since I transitioned out of my physical body.

"As I look back at my life on Earth, I realized several of my theories, like the Special and General Theories of Relativity, were ahead of their time, and a number of physicists were skeptical. But this was to be expected, as this has happened frequently over the history of scientific development. A good example of this was the heliocentric theory proposed by Copernicus that the Earth and the planets revolved around the Sun. Many considered this to be heresy when it was first brought forward, because the Church maintained the Earth was the center of the universe, and his theory was not widely accepted for many years.

"Fortunately for me, I lived at a time when they no longer imprisoned heretics for proposing new theories that contradicted the scientific establishment. Several aspects of my theories have since been proven correct through scientific experiments, although there are still a few pieces that do not seem to fit. I spent most of the later years of my life trying to explain all the forces of nature (being gravity, electromagnetism, strong nuclear, and weak nuclear) in a unified field theory, but I did not succeed in this regard."

"Now that you are here on the Spirit Side, do you now know how to develop the unified field theory that alluded you on Earth?" I wondered.

"Of course. Over here all the missing pieces fell into place, and I now know how to link all the forces of nature into one unified theory. It is actually quite simple, and I slap my forehead when I realize how close I was to finding the answers I was seeking."

"Can you tell me the what you discovered over here, so I can pass it on to the physicists on Earth?"

"I wish I could, but I am not permitted to provide the answers in such a direct manner. You see, souls in the Spirit Realm are not allowed to unduly interfere with the developments on Earth. We are bound by a directive similar to that which governs the activities of the advanced races in our galaxy, which dictates no undue influence in the affairs of inferior civilizations.

"We are allowed to help out in subtle ways, like sending intuitive thoughts and inspirational telepathic messages to humans on Earth to help them solve the problems on their own. I have been working on this with other distinguished physicists over here, and sometime in the near future our colleagues on Earth will come up with the answers."

"It must be obvious to you now that many advanced civilizations in our galaxy have mastered the art of traveling between the stars in spacecraft that make those journeys faster than the speed of light, which you had postulated was the absolute maximum speed for matter in the universe," I pondered.

"Indeed, I now know these inter-stellar travelers found a work-around to this speed barrier. The universe has numerous naturally occurring gateways or wormholes that allow matter to pass through a warp or fold in the space-time continuum so a distance of many light-years can be traversed in a very short time. The warp drive that these advanced races use creates an artificial wormhole around their spacecraft that allows them to traverse the vast distances in our galaxy with relative ease.

"Someday, scientists on Earth will develop their own

version of this warp drive, and this will propel humans on Earth to the next level of technological achievement. Hopefully by then humans on Earth will have stopped their abusive behavior, otherwise the Galactic Council will have to act to ensure they will not use the warp drive to wage war on other planets."

"Have you thought about incarnating once more as a human on Earth?" I asked.

"I have thought about it, but my inclination right now is to stay on the Spirit Side because I believe I can be more helpful to humanity by working with them from this side of the veil. Here I can work with many scientists at once by sending them helpful tips through intuitive thoughts and telepathic whispers, whereas if I return to Earth in a physical body I will be slowed down by all the distractions and limitations that happen during a human journey."

"Do you have any words of wisdom to pass on to the folks back on Earth?" I ventured.

"Humans should do what the Council of Wise Ones, Gaia, and other wise spirits have said: Discard all your negative emotions and fully embrace love, compassion, and forgiveness. If this can be achieved, Earth will become a much more pleasant and enjoyable place to live, and humanity will be ready for the next quantum leap in their technological advancement."

With a nod to us, Albert Einstein rose from the chair and ambled slowly toward the white city.

Albert then surprised me by announcing he planned to introduce me to a couple of souls who had completed lives on Earth as famous women. He said this was in response to comments I had received from readers that most of the meetings he had arranged for me on the Spirit Side were with famous men. He acknowledged that women had played major roles in the development of our civilization, but they were outnumbered by men (at least so far) due to the patriarchal nature of human societies over the ages.

I was delighted to hear this from Albert, and eagerly followed him to a small plaza in the city where I knew he would deliver on his promise.

# ᨒ Chapter Seventeen ᨑ
## *Noble Aristocrat*

Sitting under a large oak tree in the corner of the plaza was a beautiful lady dressed in a long flowing gown adorned with white lace and small blue gemstones. She smiled as we approached and motioned for us to sit on a bench opposite her chair. Albert introduced her as Maria Antonia Josepha Johanna, better known as Marie Antoinette, queen of France and wife of King Louis XVI, the last king of France before the French Revolution.

"Greetings, Your Majesty," I began. "Thank you for meeting with us today. You certainly had a fascinating life in France, until it ended abruptly when your head was sliced off in a guillotine. But there are a few holes in your history that have perplexed historians for centuries. Are you willing to talk about your life as queen of France?"

"Of course, you can ask me anything," she responded with an engaging smile.

"I will start off with the most obvious question. Some historians believe you said 'let them eat cake' when you were advised the peasants had no bread to eat. Is this true?"

"No, I never said that, and I don't know how that misconception got started. Although I lived a very pampered life, with many servants, elaborate dresses, exquisite jewelry, and decadent food to eat, I was not so pompous that I could not appreciate the dire straits of the poor people in France. Except I did not feel it was my responsibility to make things better for them, and so I let others deal (or not deal) with their plight.

"Many citizens in France thought I was arrogant and condescending, and hence I was not surprised to later learn someone had attributed that statement to me, so I would be denigrated in the eyes of the nation. As you know, royalty in France in those days had been criticized for obscene extravagance when many people had to struggle to feed their families. This was another attempt to smear my good name and label me as someone who was hopelessly out of touch with reality."

"You were born into the Hapsburg royal family, the youngest daughter of Empress Maria Theresa, who arranged your marriage with Louis-Auguste, the heir to the throne of France (later to become King Louis XVI). How did you feel about this marriage?"

"I was only fourteen when I was married and still very much of a child. I was apprehensive when my mother told me about the betrothal, because I had never met my future husband and did not know much about him. But I understood that arranged marriages were common among royal families in Europe, so I was not totally surprised when my marriage to Louis-Auguste was announced. I accepted my fate with grace and vowed to make the best of it.

"When I first met my future husband, who was fifteen at the time, I found him to be shy and reserved, but he treated me with kindness and that alleviated most of my fears. After the wedding ceremony and banquet, we were escorted by the king (Louis XV) and the archbishop of Reims to the nuptial bedchamber for the bedding ceremony. They waited patiently beside the four-poster bed for my husband and I to consummate our marriage behind the curtains. They watched with bated breath for my husband to proudly display the blood-stained sheet as confirmation our marriage had been consummated and I had been a virgin.

"But our marriage was not consummated that night, much to the disappointment of the onlookers. They attributed our failure to perform to youthful inhibitions and exhaustion after a long day. They were confident the consummation would occur in due course, although they had no idea at the time it would take seven years for this to happen.

"When we were behind the curtains of our bed, I

did what every good wife was supposed to do: I took off my nightgown and waited for my husband to penetrate me. But Louis-Auguste showed little interest in my naked body, and he was not able to achieve an erection. I did not understand at the time what the problem was, and I wondered if he did not find me sexually attractive.

"Under pressure to consummate from out families (who were embarrassed at our inability to do so), we rendezvoused every night in my bedchamber, but to no avail. I did not find out until later that my husband was gay, and he had no interest in heterosexual activities. Being a homosexual in those days was more than scandalous, as it was considered a grave sin by the Church and often led to prosecution and imprisonment. So, we kept his sexual orientation confidential and went through the nightly charade in our bedchamber to allay suspicions.

"After my husband was crowned King Louis XVI, he realized it was important for him to have an heir. So, he arranged for one of his knights to secretly join me in bed, after which the king proudly announced we had consummated our marriage. These nightly escapades continued unnoticed until his surrogate was no longer needed, having fathered all four of my children. We managed to fool everyone into believing the king had sired all the children and the line of succession had been established. It is unfortunate that because of the French

Revolution none of our children got to ascend to the throne.

"I went along with the arrangement as I understood the importance of an heir, and I did not want to disrupt the royal court and disappoint my family. The king's surrogate was a handsome young man who was a skilled lover, so I actually came to enjoy our secret liaisons. Over the years I had many other sexual partners, as did the king, and we both took this secret to our graves."

"Did you foresee the coming revolution?" I wondered.

"No, not at all. We knew the peasants were restless and unhappy, but we had no inkling things would end up the way they did. Despite warnings from his staff the king was determined to stay in France, rather than flee to safety. I felt my duty was to stay with my husband, so I remained behind as well, hoping the revolt would fizzle out and things would return to normal.

"It all happened so fast. Before we could react, the king and I were imprisoned to await trial. My husband was convicted first and was summarily executed by the guillotine. Shortly after, I was convicted of several crimes against the state, including high treason. (I firmly believe the Revolutionary Tribunal had made up its mind about my guilt before the trial.)

"Shortly after the conviction, I was led out of my

cell to the place of execution. It was a raised platform in the middle of a square with a guillotine in the center, and a cushion in front of the blade for me to kneel on. I placed my neck in the slot, and my head was neatly severed from my body when the executioner released the blade."

"Were you fearful as you walked to the guillotine? What happened after your head was chopped off?" I asked.

"I was apprehensive, of course, but my fear was alleviated to a large degree by two of my spirit guides who came to my cell a few days before my execution. I was surprised at first, but I soon felt comfortable around them, as I basked in the glow of their unconditional love. They said they would be with me all the way, and when I left my body they would escort me to the Spirit Side.

"They walked with me to the guillotine, but only I could see them. I left my body just before the blade was released, so I did not feel any pain. Once I was out of my body, I felt an amazing sense of lightness and freedom, and with great pleasure I followed my guides up toward the bright light. I glanced back once to say good-bye to my body and watched as my head rolled off the platform and into the gutter."

"Do you have any regrets about that life?" I asked.

"Hell, yes. I have many regrets, but I chalk it all up to another journey as a human on Earth. Obviously, we should have taken the unrest of the commoners more seriously and made the changes to society that would have quelled the rebellion. Had we done that, it is likely the French monarchy could have survived, just like the monarchy in Britain. Or, at the very least, we should have fled the country to live out our lives in exile.

"No one is perfect, and I made a lot of mistakes, but I hope to learn from those mistakes so I can continue my growth and evolution."

We both gave Marie a farewell hug and watched the elegant lady leave the plaza. Before I could make any comment to Albert, I noticed our next guest arriving from the other side of the plaza. She was an elderly lady dressed in a simple white cotton sari with a blue border. Albert introduced her as Mother Teresa, also known as Saint Teresa of Calcutta.

# Chapter Eighteen
## *Earth Angel*

"Greetings, Mother Teresa," Albert began. "I brought a friend to meet you, as he is doing research for his next book."

"Welcome to you both," she said with a bright smile. "How can I be of service?"

"I am honored to meet you, Mother Teresa," I responded. "You certainly led an exemplary life on Earth, earning many accolades, including winning the Nobel Peace Prize and being canonized as a saint by Pope Francis. How do you feel about your life on Earth now that you can view it with the benefit of hindsight?"

Mother Teresa seemed to be lost in thought, as she contemplated my question. After several minutes of silence, she began: "After I crossed over, I found my Life Review to be a real eye-opener. People on Earth do not realize how little they remember about their lives until they can view it in intimate detail during their Life Review. Our human minds tend to store only a small number of the events in our lives in our conscious memories, and usually this includes only the more significant happenings we have experienced.

"In a Life Review, we get to fill in the gaps of our human memories, and often these seemingly minor events take on a much greater importance than we could have imagined. As the old saying goes: 'the devil is in the details' and looking at the details of one's life can reveal some surprising insights, both good and bad.

"The ability of the human mind to 'forget' the minutiae of our lives is a valid defense mechanism. Otherwise, our minds would be way too cluttered with memories that would make it difficult to function on a day-to-day basis. It is similar to why we are not allowed to remember our past lives while on Earth—because such memories would be an unbearable burden that would unduly interfere with our human journeys. Imagine how difficult it would be for a person to carry on a normal life if they were able to recall all the terrible things they did to others in previous lives, or to remember all the pain, suffering, and injustice they had to endure in past lives.

"Most souls who incarnate on Earth have had many lives in different situations, which we chose for ourselves to grow and evolve as souls. And you can be certain not all our lives have been 'saintly.' In some lives, we may have been cruel brutes who inflicted pain, suffering, and death on others, while in other journeys we were the victims of such abuse. And in other lives we may have managed to rise above the fray to selflessly attend to the well-being of our fellow humans. No human life is perfect, but some have more shortcomings than others.

"When we return to the Spirit Side in our natural state as beings of energy, those memories of our past lives, and the intimate details of our most recent lives on Earth, are merely objective observations about our journeys in a physical body, without any feelings of guilt, remorse, or judgment. Our journeys on Earth are designed to be a learning experience—a way to enhance our knowledge about ourselves and the universe, and to gain the wisdom we need to put it all into perspective.

"When I look back at my life as Mother Teresa, I can see a number of the glaring flaws in my actions that weren't apparent to me or the public. I do acknowledge I made a positive difference to most people, but overall, I was hardly a 'saint.' I am amused by the praise that was heaped on me by the Catholic Church, and especially by my canonization as Saint Teresa. Although on balance I believe I did more good than harm, I was no different from thousands of other people through the ages who toiled in obscurity to help others in an effort to make the world a better place.

"I was canonized mainly because my efforts caught the attention of the media, who were eager to promote my works as an example of something good that happened in a world beset by violence, crime, and poverty. And with all this worldly attention, the Catholic Church was under pressure to honor me in a special way, and so they jumped through all the hoops to make me a saint to satisfy the clamor from the masses.

"What is a saint, anyway? In my view, it is a long out-dated anachronism, like so many other tenets of the Church. Originally it was designed to honor faithful Christians who performed exceptionally good deeds (including at least two verifiable 'miracles') in the service of the Church. It was a way to tell the masses that faithfully following the rules and dogmas of the Church, and praying fervently to the Lord, could lead the way to a certain path into Heaven. And so being canonized was like being inducted into the Christian Hall of Fame.

"The truth is, every soul is an individual aspect of the Source, a being of energy without imperfections that can easily perform 'miracles' without even breaking a sweat. But a soul incarnated in a physical body must deal with the limitations of its human form. To state someone is a saint is really saying the person has been able to emulate some of the inherent qualities all souls enjoy without any special effort.

"So, am I a saint? Yes, I am, but so is Albert and all the other good souls in the Spirit Realm. And you are as well, Garnet, except it doesn't show up very much while you are still having a human journey on Earth. When you transition over to the Spirit Side, I will be sure to call you Saint Garnet," she said with a twinkle in her eye, as she bade us farewell.

"Don't let this go to your head," Albert cautioned. "You are still having a human journey on Earth, and we both know you are far from being saintly. In fact, as I watch your antics every day, I shake my head in disbelief and wonder how I let you sign me up to be one of your guides. If I promise to deliver you a bacon cheeseburger every day for the rest of your life, will you let me out of my contract?"

"Of course, Albert. But only if you throw in fries with gravy as well."

Albert rolled his eyes and beckoned me to follow him. I left with an extra spring in my step as I contemplated what Mother Teresa had told me. I wondered if someone on Earth would name a church after me …

# ◈ Chapter Nineteen ◈
## *Escape from the Hellhole*

The only guarantee in life is death and taxes. From the moment we are born we are in the process of dying, because every day takes us closer to the day our physical bodies will perish and die. No person on Earth can escape the inevitable, no matter how rich or powerful they may be. Death is the great equalizer, as we all leave this planet as beings of energy, taking nothing with us except the memories of the lives we just finished. The movie stars, sports heroes, billionaires, and homeless people all end up back on the Spirit Side regardless of what they did on Earth or how they lived their lives.

Many people fear death, mainly because they don't know what will happen to them after they die, they are afraid of dying alone, or they dread a painful or terrifying demise. These fears are understandable, but without merit, as Albert has made clear in his revelations about the cycle of reincarnation on Earth.

To reinforce his teachings, on one of my trips to the Spirit Side Albert took me to watch the arrival of a soul who had just finished her life as a middle-aged lady who died from cancer. I watched with fascination as Sarah rose from the hospital escorted by three of her spirit guides. As soon as she arrived at the lush meadow in front of the white city of Aglaia, she was greeted by a group of souls who welcomed her with open arms and warm, loving hugs. In this group were her parents, grandparents, aunts and uncles, a few close friends who had predeceased her, as well as her beloved Muffy, a blue point Siamese cat who had been put down several months before. Sarah was delighted to see these souls once again, as she basked in the glow of their unconditional love.

When the group eventually dispersed, I caught up with Sarah as she headed to the Akashic Records for her Life Review.

"Pardon me, Sarah, I would like to ask you a few questions. My name is Garnet, and this is one of my spirit guides, Albert."

"So nice to meet you both. What would you like to know?"

"I understand you died from cancer, and you were in hospice care for the last couple of months. Please tell me about your last days on Earth. Were you in pain? Did you feel all alone? Were you scared of dying?"

"I would be happy to answer your questions," Sarah responded, "as I hope my story will provide a bit of comfort to those people back on Earth who are also near the end.

"Until the cancer reared its ugly head, I was a successful lawyer with a busy practice and many satisfied clients. I had been happily married to a wonderful man for thirty-six years, and we both enjoyed family time with our two daughters, their partners, and our three darling grandchildren. My life was about as good as it gets, until the grim reaper tapped me on the shoulder and told me the end was near.

"Before cancer rained on my parade, I had been healthy as a horse, never having spent a day in the hospital (except for the birth of my daughters). The diagnosis from my doctor hit me like a ton of bricks, and I went through all the usual emotional stages of a terminal patient: denial, anger, bargaining, depression, and acceptance.

"I had been raised as a Christian but had long since given up on religion, as I became an affirmed agnostic. I had been so wrapped up in my professional career and the joys of family life that I seldom turned my mind to the question of what would become of me when I died. Only after the onset of cancer did I seriously consider this question, and then I was at a total loss for answers. Surely, I thought (and hoped) there must be some part of me that continues after death, although I feared I could be wrong, and I would disappear into nothingness as soon as my body perished.

"In desperation, I read the Bible and books on spirituality, searching for comfort. In the end, I concluded that the Heaven/Hell paradigm promoted by the Christian Church did not make any sense, but I did resonate with the teachings of the spiritual gurus who presented an alternate vision of life, death, and the afterlife. I sincerely hoped they were right, but I harbored some misgivings about the veracity of their philosophy, and these doubts caused me much discomfort.

"Many nights I would wake up in a cold sweat, trembling at the prospect of a slow, painful death, followed by a dark and lonely nonexistence. Surely, I silently pleaded, this must be a terrible dream, and I will wake up to continue with my happy life as it was before the cancer struck.

"I had lots of loving support from my family, who came to see me every day, but they could not give me the assurance I was seeking. In fact, no one could give me the comfort I desperately needed, until Selene appeared in my life.

"It happened one night when I woke up after a terrifying nightmare. I saw a beautiful lady standing at the foot of my bed dressed in a long white robe, with a smile that lit up the whole room. She told me her name was Selene and she was one of my spirit guides who had been with me since birth. Her loving, calm demeanor put me at ease, and I felt an amazing sense of peace in her presence.

"Although I knew from my spiritual research that we were all supposed to have spirit guides, I had never before been aware of my guides, and I had concerns about whether they really existed. But Selene slayed all my doubts quickly as she explained who she was and why she had appeared in my hospital room.

"She told me the things I had read in the spiritual books were more or less true, and I should not fear death because it was a doorway to another world where I would enjoy peace, happiness, and boundless unconditional love. She said she would be at my side until I left my body even though my family would not be able to see her. She cautioned me against mentioning her to the staff or my family, so they would not think I had become demented.

"Selene told me no one dies alone, as our spirit guides are always with us to provide comfort and guidance as the end draws near. It is the goal of our spirit guides to make the transition out of our bodies as easy as possible.

"Selene made my last days on Earth much more bearable. She was at my side 24/7, constantly reassuring me that the transition would be painless, and I would be delighted to be rid of my cancer-wracked body once I left it behind. She worked her magic, and I felt no pain or discomfort during the run-up to the demise of my body.

"When my body finally gave up the ghost, I easily slipped out of it and began hovering above my bed. I could see my human body lying motionless, surrounded by my family. They were quietly weeping in their grief, even though they had known for a long time this moment was coming. I wanted to reach out to assure them I was very much alive and well, but they could not hear or see me. I was saddened by the prospect of leaving my family behind, but at the same time I was exhilarated with my newfound freedom. I was no longer bound by the limitations of my physical body, and I now understood my true nature as an eternal being of energy.

"Then Selene tapped me on the shoulder and said it was time to move on. She took me by the hand, and we rose up through the ceiling toward a bright light in the distance. We were joined by two of my other guides who smothered me with loving hugs, as they helped Selene escort me through the bright light to a lush meadow on the other side, where I met my welcoming party."

"That is quite a touching story, Sarah. Do you have any words of wisdom for the people who will read about your adventures in my book?'

"First and foremost, remember you are never alone, even when it seems there is no one else around. Your guides are always with you, and they will make themselves visible near the end to comfort and guide you through the transition out of your body to the Spirit Side. And just as important, you can rest assured you will not feel any pain or discomfort during your transition.

"Leaving one's body and transitioning to the Spirit Side is like a caterpillar emerging from its chrysalis as a beautiful butterfly and flying off in the sunlight. It is an ecstatic transformation that cannot be adequately described in words. So do not fear death, because what lays beyond is the pot of gold at the end of the rainbow."

"Thank you so much, Sarah. We will leave you now to enjoy your Life Review."

We waved farewell to Sarah as she followed her guides to the Hall of Records that housed the Akashic Records, where we knew she would be able to review the human life she had left behind.

Albert and I waited outside the Hall of Records for Sarah to emerge after finishing her Life Review. She strolled happily toward us, with a smile on her face, and greeted us warmly: "Hello once again, Albert and Garnet. Do you wish to ask me more questions?"

"Please tell us how your Life Review went. What did you learn?" I asked Sarah.

"My Life Review was awesome. I got to look back on my life on Earth in minute increments, and it was very enlightening. I was able to clearly understand why I made all the mistakes I made on my journey, and what I could have done to avoid hurting other people. And I was able to access the details of the Life Plan I made before I incarnated, so I could get a clear picture of where I veered off course.

"One of the most profound aspects of a Life Review is the ability to hear the thoughts and feel the emotions of the people I interacted with during my journey. So when I came to the part where I had chided my husband about forgetting our wedding anniversary, I got to feel his shame and anguish over his memory lapse, which I now know happened because he was dealing with a crisis at work that occupied all his time and energy for several weeks. I wish he was here now, so I could offer him an apology for being so selfish.

"Thankfully, I also got to review some of the good things I did on Earth, and to bask in the love and gratitude of those people on the receiving end of my generosity. I never realized how much I had been appreciated when I took a basket of freshly baked cookies to my father every day when he was living his last years in a seniors' home. I could feel his deep gratitude that I was such a thoughtful and caring daughter, and this brought tears to my eyes.

"The good news is that a Life Review is not intended to make a soul feel bad about their mistakes, or to instill a false sense of pride about the goods things a soul may have accomplished. Its primary purpose is to be a learning tool for the soul, to help it plan its next incarnation. No one judges a soul for what it did, except the soul itself, and no one will criticize a soul for its wrong turns or abusive behavior, because all souls understand the challenges faced by every soul who incarnates on the Earth plane.

"I now understand the challenges I had hoped to overcome and the lessons I needed to learn from my life as Sarah, and I know how I measured up to the goals I had set for myself. My job now is to meet with the Council to discuss my next move."

We followed Sarah to the Hall of Wisdom and entered the room where the members of the Council were seated around a table in the shape of a horseshoe. The Chair of the Council, Sophia, spoke to Sarah in a soothing voice: "Welcome back, Sarah. Now that you have finished your Life Review, what would you like to do next? As you know, you have had several hundred lives on Earth, and you are free to choose your next course of action. The Council is here to help you make an informed decision, but you have the final say on what happens next. You can plan another incarnation on Earth or on another planet with life forms, explore the universe as a being of energy, or stay on the Spirit Side for as long as you want to relax."

"I don't think I have learned enough yet to graduate from the Earth school," Sarah responded. "My inclination is to plan another journey on Earth as a human, and this time I hope to overcome all my challenges and gain valuable knowledge and wisdom in the process.

"When I was living on Earth, I used to swear an oath to myself that, if reincarnation was for real, there was no way I would return to this Hellhole. In my view back then, Earth was a cesspool of harsh conditions, pain and suffering, and out-of-control negative emotions. But I now see things from a much different perspective, and I have changed my mind," Sarah announced proudly.

"So be it, Sarah," Sophia responded. "We accept your plan, as we think another life on Earth would be beneficial for you. When you are ready, I suggest you spend some time in a Life Planning session with the members of your soul group. We will review and comment on your new Life Plan when you are ready, and then you will be all set for your next adventure."

The members of the Council rose and slowly filed out of the room, while Sarah strode out of the Hall of Wisdom with a renewed sense of purpose. As I contemplated what Sarah had said, I wondered what choice I would make after my current human journey ended. Albert seemed to sense what I was thinking, so he told me to relax because I could jump off that bridge when I came to it. Thank you, Albert, for such sage advice.

As I waited for Albert to make his next move, I

recalled Albert Einstein's mention of ET races that can travel between the stars, and this reminded me of one of my early conversations with Albert about the universe. When I asked him if there was life on other planets, he just rolled his eyes and asked me if I thought the Source had created all the stars in the sky merely to give humans something pretty to admire at night. I hadn't really thought much about it, but I blushed with embarrassment when I realized how silly my question had been. (In hindsight, I now realize this was another of many stupid questions I had posed to Albert over the course of our relationship.) And I let my mind drift back to that occasion when Albert patiently explained to me the reality of extraterrestrial life.

# ᨒChapter Twenty ᨓ
## *Life in the Cosmos*

In that earlier conversation Albert assured me there were billions and billions of different life forms existing not just in our galaxy, but in all the countless galaxies that were part of the observable universe. He noted that a number of these life forms were much more intelligent and more technologically advanced than humans on Earth, and many of these ET races had the ability to travel between the stars. He advised that a number of them have been observing the developments on our planet for aeons, and they continue to do so to this very day.

To reinforce his point, Albert took me to meet a humanoid ET living on a spacecraft orbiting our planet.

"Greetings to you, Albert, and to your companion from Earth," the ET announced telepathically. "Our species has been visiting Earth for millions of years, even before it had any life. The Galactic Council sent us initially to confirm Earth was suitable for life, and, when we advised them in the affirmative, the Council enlisted our help to begin the long process of seeding life on Earth.

We started with primitive life forms from other planets in the galaxy, followed by more and more advanced life forms. Eventually, we seeded the planet with humans.

"Our mandate was to assist with the evolution and development of all forms of life on Earth, except we were not allowed to directly interfere with the events on the planet. Our assistance was much more subtle—we could teach humans new techniques to help them move forward and we could use our technology here and there to improve their way of life. For the most part, however, we were passive observers.

"As a result of the noninterference directive, we were forced to sit on the sidelines and watch several of your highly evolved civilizations, like Atlantis and Lemuria, rise up to their glory days before collapsing. Tragically, these civilizations lost sight of their core values and succumbed to their negative emotions. They let the dark side of humanity triumph over love, and they paid the price. Every time this happened, the humans who survived the destruction had to start over again. It was difficult for us to watch these events, although we always held out the hope that the human experiment on Earth would eventually work out.

"Now humans have once again reached an advanced stage of development, a level which they can use as the launch pad to raise their vibrations and achieve a higher level of consciousness. And we have seen a lot of progress in this regard in the last few decades as more and more humans are rejecting the dark side in favor of enlightenment. But not all humans are in the same place, and progress on this front seems unduly slow at times.

"The foremost concern we have is that humans have developed technology that is capable of destroying all life on Earth. Nuclear bombs, chemical and biological weapons, and other weapons of mass destruction are products of the dark side of humanity—the side that fosters fear, anger, hatred, and greed.

"We have the capability to destroy all your weapons, but we are not allowed to do so. The shift to enlightenment must be done by humans themselves, with a little help from their friends. Ever since humans first split the atom during World War II, Earth has attracted the attention of many other ET races who are now watching the activities on Earth. They too cannot directly interfere with events on Earth, although they are also working quietly behind the scenes to help humans. All the ET species have worked closely with the Council of Wise Ones, who have been coordinating all the activities to encourage humans to discard the darkness and embrace the light. And the pace and intensity of these efforts has increased markedly in recent years.

"We are in the middle of a full-court press with

humanity because the time for action is upon us. We are determined to use every effort we can muster to ensure your civilization does not destroy itself, but we need all the help we can get.

"We carefully monitor all activity on your planet to detect situations that might lead to disputes or conflicts with the potential to escalate out of control. In these cases, our goal is to scale back the hostilities with a program of intense telepathic thoughts beamed at those humans who can calm the discord and spread the peace. This has not always worked in the past, but we continue to improve our techniques to target the right people with our plea to discard fear and anger and embrace love and compassion.

"Right now, as in the past, with the use of our advanced technology, some members of our race are living on Earth disguised as humans. You have likely encountered these pseudo-humans many times in the past without being aware of their true identities. Their mission is to exert a positive influence on the humans around them through their words and actions so more and more humans will shun the darkness and welcome the light.

"As well, we have enlisted a few of your people, directly or by telepathy, to communicate our message of hope to other humans via interpersonal contacts and broad dissemination through various media channels. This is why Albert brought you here. We want you to communicate our aspirations for humanity as part of our master plan. You are only one small cog in a very large wheel—but every little bit helps."

Well, that certainly explained the basis for the numerous UFO sightings that have occurred over the history of humankind. These so-called Unidentified Flying Objects are actually the spacecraft used by the various ET races to explore and monitor activities on Earth.

Albert explained that they have avoided open and direct contact with humans because they feel total disclosure at this time would be too disruptive to our civilization, possibly resulting in panic, riots, and rebellion against secular authorities and governments on Earth.

And because governments on Earth agree that such disclosure could be dangerous at this stage of human development, they have been actively conducting a cover-up campaign to keep the public in the dark. This is why the scientific establishment, encouraged by civil authorities, denies the existence of spacecraft from other planets and dismisses the reports of sightings as nothing more than natural phenomena or man-made objects like airplanes or weather balloons.

Albert assured me that these technologically advanced ET races pose no danger to humans because they are all benevolent creatures who are here to observe the activities on Earth without causing humans any harm or instigating a major upheaval of our civilization. They have no intention of conquering our planet or in killing or enslaving our people. Their technology is so advanced that they could have vanquished humankind long ago if that had been their game plan.

All the very advanced races (being the ones who have developed interstellar travel) in our galaxy belong to the Galactic Federation, whose members elect the Galactic Council. The Council enacts rules and regulations to govern the conduct of its members, with the overall intent to preserve peaceful relations among its members and to ensure that primitive and barbarous civilizations in our galaxy do not spread their violence and aggression beyond their own planets.

One of the most important rules they have implemented is the directive that no one should unduly interfere with the natural development of any other civilization, very similar to the "Prime Directive" referred to in the *Star Trek* movies and TV shows. This means the ETs who have been observing Earth are not permitted to use their advanced technology to stop our wars and aggression or destroy our weapons, which would make our world much safer and happier than the state of affairs we currently endure.

Instead, they must watch the happenings on Earth without being able to interfere to save our butts. But they can provide subtle assistance to help us develop better technology to make life easier for the denizens of our troubled planet. This help comes in the form of sending telepathic and intuitive messages to certain humans at crucial points in time to inspire them to invent new technology that helped us progress from the Stone Age to where we are now. They had to be careful to avoid helping us develop technology we were not capable of handling in a way that was beneficial, and not detrimental, to all humans.

Albert said the ETs wanted to make life easier for humans so they would not need to devote all their time finding food and shelter for their families. They knew it would be difficult for humans to expand their consciousness if they had to struggle every day just to survive. Starving humans are not able to sit quietly to listen to Spirit, since their overriding focus is to find food to alleviate their hunger pangs.

From time to time throughout our history the ETs have helped humans find new ways to raise their standard of living. They taught humans how to grow their own food, become better hunters and foragers, and make better tools and hunting weapons. With guidance from the ETs, humans learned how to organize their societies so individuals could specialize in a trade or profession and barter with other humans for food and essentials. Hundreds of our noteworthy inventions, like the printing press, microscopes, penicillin, electric lights, and telephones, to name a few, were inspired by our off-world benefactors.

Historically, most of this assistance has been very subtle. Quite often these aliens would disguise themselves as humans so they could be of service without being conspicuous. They would send telepathic messages to gifted people to inspire the development of groundbreaking inventions that boosted our technology to the next level. Occasionally they landed in their starships and used their superior technology to move large stones to build pyramids and other massive structures. Many of these encounters have been described in our holy books as miracles performed by angels.

Unfortunately, some of the help humans got from the ETs was used for the wrong purpose—to enable a few men to subjugate and kill other humans to satisfy their thirst for money and power. Since the ETs were not allowed to directly intervene, they could only stand by and watch the bloodshed with dismay. Albert maintains they still have high hopes humans will eventually make the quantum leap up to the next level.

And so we find ourselves in our current state of affairs, where we are subject to frequent wars, armed conflicts, genocide, mass shootings, and other violent crimes, mainly because our emotional and spiritual intelligence has not kept pace with our technological advances.

Albert assures me that sometime in our future (and he will not give me a time frame) the ETs will make full and open disclosure of their existence and the reason they are monitoring our progress. This will happen only when they are comfortable humans will accept this news with equanimity. And to prepare us for this momentous occasion, they have deliberately stepped up the pace of UFO sightings to condition humans to accept the fact that UFOs are really ET spacecraft from other planets.

As I struggled to digest all this information, Albert said he wanted me to see yet another ET civilization that functioned differently from humans on Earth, as part of my cosmological education. As usual, I was keen to learn as much as I could about the universe, and I hoped I would not be disappointed as I followed Albert toward a planet several light years from Earth.

# Chapter Twenty-One
## *See You Later, Alligator*

As we approached the planet from space, I could see it had land masses, oceans and lakes, and white clouds suspended in small clumps in the atmosphere. I noticed three moons orbiting this beautiful globe, and I imagined how spectacular the view would be when all three filled the night sky.

I trailed Albert as we descended toward a large land mass in the northern hemisphere. We touched down in a verdant meadow filled with lush green vegetation that was different from anything I had seen on Earth. The meadow was bordered on one side by a sparkling green lake, and on the other by a forest of towering plants that resembled nothing I had ever seen before on Earth or on any of the planets I had visited with Albert.

Overhead was a reddish-yellow sun that appeared to be about three times the size of our Sun when viewed from the surface of Earth. The sky had a pink tinge overlaying the light blue background, and the fluffy white clouds reflected the brilliant sunlight streaming from the giant sun.

The meadow appeared to be barren of all life forms, until Albert pointed toward the lake, and I could see a creature emerging from the water and striding onto the beach. It appeared to be a large reptile, resembling an alligator, as it walked upright on large hind legs using its stubby tail for balance. Its long jaw was filled with rows of razor-sharp teeth, and its large yellow eyes stared at us intently, as though it were trying to determine if we would make a tasty dinner.

I took my cue from Albert and remained motionless as we stared back at this creature from the deep. Finally, Albert broke the spell with a warm greeting: "Sobek, so nice to see again. I have brought someone to see you. His name is Garnet, and he is a human from Earth."

Sobek flashed a toothy smile and responded: "I am delighted to see you again, Albert. It has been a long time. How can I be of service today?"

"Garnet is an author who has been writing books about the wonders of the universe, and I thought it would be useful for him to meet with you. Do you have time to answer a few questions?"

"Of course, I always have time for you, Albert."

I recalled what Albert had told me before we journeyed to this planet. Apparently, Albert and Sobek had lived a previous life together on Earth in the sixteenth century in Spain. Albert had been the captain of a galleon in the Spanish navy and Sobek had been his wife. They had fallen in love as teenagers and went on to be married soon after they first met. Albert said it was love at first sight, and he had truly adored his wife and their two children.

He had managed to survive numerous conflicts at sea, and finally settled down to retire with his family in a small fishing village on the southern coast of Spain. He died peacefully of old age, with Sobek and their children at his bedside. After a pleasant transition to the Spirit Side, he had waited patiently to welcome Sobek when she finally left her human body behind. After a brief sojourn on the Spirit Side, Sobek decided to try her luck in a different venue and incarnated as a reptilian on this planet. She and Albert had stayed in touch telepathically, but this was the first face-to-face meeting since she began her journey on this planet.

"Tell me about life on this planet, Sobek. It would seem to be much different from your last life on Earth."

"Life here is very different, and way more enjoyable. After many lives on Earth, this planet is a breath of fresh air. Here we have a very balanced ecosystem with no pollution and the dominant species, of which I am one, does not subjugate or abuse the other creatures who share our planet.

"My race has similar physical characteristics to the reptiles on Earth, as we were both seeded from the same planet by the advanced ET races. And because we don't have any humans on our world, my race was able to develop naturally without interference from another dominant race.

"As a result, my species has a larger brain than any of the reptiles on Earth, and, in many respects, we are more intelligent than humans on your planet. We communicate with each other by telepathy, and we understand our connection to the Source and to each other. It would be unthinkable for us to cause any harm to other members of our race or to the other creatures on our planet. We live simple lives close to nature and understand everything on this planet, both animate and inanimate, has its own special place in the universe.

"Although we don't have much technology, and have no need for it, we have developed unique energy-conversion technology that allows us to transform light energy from our sun into energy our bodies can use as sustenance. This allows our bodies to receive all necessary nutrients from our sun, and we don't need to consume animal flesh or even vegetation in order to survive. Although we might look similar to the alligators on Earth, we are not carnivores and if you were here in physical form you would not have to worry about me having you for dinner."

"Please tell me more about your energy-conversion technology. It sounds like this could make life on any planet less violent and more harmonious," I queried.

"It was developed by our scientists long ago, but only after a lot of trial and error. As you know, everything is energy, in one form or another, and this technology transforms the light energy emanating from our sun into molecular energy that provides nourishment to our bodies. The closest analogy would be the process of photosynthesis on Earth, wherein plants convert light energy from your sun into chemical energy that sustains the plants.

"Collecting the light energy was the easy part, as we have large solar panels to catch the sun's rays, not unlike the solar panels you have on Earth. The tricky part was to develop a system that could convert this energy into something that could nourish our bodies. After many failed attempts, we learned how to do so by passing a beam of light through a crystal with a unique molecular structure. When the beam of energy emerges from the crystal it has special properties that allow it to be absorbed by our skin and converted into the nutrients we need to sustain healthy bodies. This is like the way sunlight on Earth is converted to vitamin D when absorbed by human skin, but our process is much more complex.

"As a result, we do not need to eat food of any kind, not even plant-based food. Once each day we go into radiation chambers to be bathed in this special energy, and this is all we need to sustain strong and healthy bodies. It beats the heck out of hunting other animals and eating their flesh, and it allows us to be paragons of virtue as regards the other animals on our planet."

"This is certainly a fascinating story," I concluded. "I am wondering if you can tell me the secret to this process, so I can pass it on to the scientists on Earth. It would be a quantum leap for humans on my planet, and a huge relief for all the animals who are slaughtered every day to feed hungry homo sapiens."

"I was forewarned by Albert that you would ask me that question, but unfortunately this is not possible. As we are a member of the Galactic Federation, we must adhere to their prime directive that we not unduly interfere with the development of an inferior race. In their view, humans on Earth are an inferior race, and we must allow things on Earth to develop in their own way without giving them advanced technology they are not ready to use in a peaceful manner. The process we use to nourish our bodies could be used for nefarious purposes in the hands of evil men, who could easily transform it into a death ray to kill other people and animals.

"Someday, when humans on Earth learn to discard their violent and abusive ways and embrace love and compassion for all living things, we may be able to share this secret with the people on your planet so it will be used only for benevolent purposes. Your fellow humans have a long way to go to reach this point, but it can be done.

"Good luck to you, Garnet, on your quest to enlighten your fellow humans. Never give up on this noble crusade because the very survival of your race is at stake."

"Thank you, Sobek, for sharing your story. I hope someday we will meet again, either on the physical plane or in the Spirit Realm."

"You are most welcome to incarnate on this planet," Sobek ventured. "I think you would look good in alligator skin, and it would be a marked improvement from your current Pillsbury doughboy appearance."

I winced as Sobek gave us a toothy smile, and Albert chuckled at my discomfort. As I followed Albert up through the clouds on our way back to Earth, I felt certain I would never view alligators on Earth in the same way again.

I smiled as I recalled the encounter we had with the reptilian ET. Before that, Albert had shown me several different ET civilizations on planets many light years from Earth, and I no longer harbor any doubts about other life in the universe. But I was curious about the technology of the advanced ET races, and I wondered if there wasn't a way for our civilization to accelerate the development of our technology to allow us to explore the stars just like Captain Kirk.

I was especially curious about Area 51 in Nevada, which some people believe to be home to super secretive projects and experiments conducted by the US military. I knew from one of my visits to the Akashic Records with Albert that the spacecraft that crashed into the New Mexico desert in 1947 had been taken there, and I wondered what had become of the spacecraft.

When I got the chance, I posed the question to Albert, hoping he could shed light on the topic.

# ༼Chapter Twenty-Two ༽
## *Cavern in the Desert*

"I have a question for you, Albert, about Area 51 in Nevada. I have read several 'conspiracy theories' about this air force base, and I would like to know the true story about what is hidden there and what projects or experiments are happening at this very secretive installation. Some people believe this base houses ET spacecraft and even bodies of aliens. What can you tell me about Area 51?"

"I knew you would get around to asking this question eventually," Albert responded. "The best way to answer your question is to take you there on one of our astral trips."

Without further ado, Albert led the way to Nevada where we briefly hovered over Area 51 before dropping down to the surface. (No one noticed us, because we were traveling in astral form, which made us invisible and undetectable to the people on the base.) We strolled toward one of the small sheds nearby and passed through the steel door blocking the entrance. Inside was an elevator with the door closed, which we passed through easily and then drifted down the shaft to the very bottom, several hundred feet below the surface.

We glided through the steel door at the bottom and entered a large underground cavern bustling with activity. Uniformed military personnel were everywhere, and they all seemed to be busy carrying out their assigned tasks with grim determination.

Albert led me to a large concrete building with armed guards posted on either side of the large steel door. On one side of the door was a small rectangular box Albert said was a retina scanning device used to allow authorized persons to enter the building. We passed through the door like it was made of vapor, and my jaw dropped when I saw what was inside.

It was a large disk, about fifty feet in diameter, with a bulge in the center about twenty feet thick. The outer edge of the disk was punctuated with a row of round portholes, but I could not see any other markings on its smooth surface. It was made of a shiny black metal that reflected the light from the halogen lamps overhead. On the lower part of the bulge was a rectangular opening, which appeared to be a doorway to the inside. It reminded me of the depictions of "flying saucers" I had seen over the years.

I peered through the doorway and the inside of the craft looked like the cockpit of the space shuttle. There were three padded chairs aligned in a row in front of the instrument panel.

"What is it?" I asked Albert. "It looks like the spacecraft that crashed near Roswell, New Mexico, in 1947. I recall you taking me to watch the crash in the Akashic Records on one of our trips to the Spirit Side."

"It is indeed," he responded. "This spacecraft was piloted by ETs from the planet Gorgon, in the Pieces constellation. They were part of an observation vanguard that had been monitoring Earth ever since the first fission bomb exploded, which had attracted the attention of this alien civilization. Their mission was to observe the activities of humans and report their findings to their superiors on their home planet. This spacecraft was a scouting vehicle based on a large mother ship orbiting the Earth.

"The little scout craft had been on a reconnaissance mission to observe a high-altitude surveillance balloon launched by the US military as part of a top-secret program named Mogul. As it approached the balloon at a high speed, its advanced propulsion system inexplicably failed, causing it to crash into the balloon payload. The collision knocked out an essential component of the craft's guidance system, which caused the spacecraft to crash into the desert below.

"As you saw in the Akashic Records, the military

denied the existence of a flying saucer (despite several eyewitness accounts to the contrary), and when they displayed the crash debris to the press it was indeed the wreckage from the balloon, as they claimed. What they didn't disclose, however, was the existence of the saucer that had crashed a few miles from the site of the balloon wreckage.

"The spacecraft was transported under heavy security to Roswell Army Airfield, then to Edwards Air Force Base, and finally to its resting place here in Area 51, where it remains hidden to this very day. The saucer was constructed of a super-strength metallic alloy that allowed it to survive the crash without major structural damage. The scientists have extensively analyzed the alloy, but they have not yet been able to decipher its composition. Likewise, they have not been able to understand the nature of its propulsion or avionic systems. In short, the military engineers have still not been able to figure out how this spacecraft functioned.

"As for the crew of the scout craft, two of them died on impact from injuries to their internal organs. The third one survived for several days, eventually succumbing to its injuries despite the valiant attempts of the medical team at the airfield. Their internal organs were not too dissimilar to those of humans, but the damage had been too extensive, and they had not been able to save the little guy.

"All three corpses were flown to Edwards Air Force Base where autopsies were performed. Later the bodies, still immersed in preservative chemicals, were transported to Area 51 where they remain today.

"The existence of the spacecraft and its crew has been denied by the US government ever since the 1947 crash. The cover-up was authorized initially by high-ranking military officers, and all subsequent US government administrations have continued the blackout on the basis the public did not need to know the truth."

"Have the scientists tried to operate the craft or reverse engineer it in order to build a similar ship?" I asked Albert.

"Ever since it arrived here, they have been trying to figure how the craft operated. They pushed all the buttons and flicked all the switches, but to no avail. They could not even figure out how to open and close the door. The instrument panel is seamless, with no obvious way to take it apart to see what is inside. They even tried to cut a hole in the panel, but the material was impervious to the best drills and saws available, and they did not even make a dent.

"They swabbed the panel with concentrated hydrochloric acid and burned it with an acetylene torch, but nothing could penetrate this material. The same was true for the metal forming the hull of the craft.

"As time marched on, the scientists had access to more advanced technologies, but not even ultrasound, CT scans, MRI, or powerful laser beams could penetrate the inside of the panel or the metallic hull. The engineers here would love to decipher the inner workings of this craft so they could build one themselves, but the craft has kept its secrets intact to this very day.

"Imagine what an advantage the US military would have if it could manufacture spacecraft similar to this one. Maybe that is good, because this type of craft could upset the world order if it fell into the wrong hands."

"Do you know the composition of the ship's hull and instrument panel?" I asked Albert.

"They are made from a metallurgical alloy that takes advanced technological sophistication to produce. Currently, scientists on Earth do not have the capability to produce this alloy, even if they were able to figure out its composition. But someday in the future humans on Earth will be able to replicate this material."

"No doubt you will not be allowed to hand over the formula to Earth scientists because of the prime directive," I surmised.

"You are right. We cannot give them the formula for the alloy on a silver platter, but we can send intuitive messages to lead them in the right direction. However, this process is quite slow because most of the messages we send to the scientists get lost in the jumble of everyday thoughts."

"What about their propulsion system? Do you know how it works?" I wondered.

"It is a combination of an antigravity generator, which can nullify the effect of gravity on the ship, and a particle beam thruster to propel the ship at great speeds. This type of propulsion system is also used by the mother ship, when it is not in warp drive, to allow maneuvering in close quarters. Scientists on Earth are still years away from developing these systems, but they will eventually get there, and they will use these propulsion systems to travel to other planets and moons in your solar system long before they develop a warp drive to travel to other stars."

"What about the three aliens who had piloted this craft? Where are their bodies?" I prodded Albert.

"Come with me. I will show you," Albert responded, as he led me into another concrete building not far from the scout craft. Inside this building I noticed two glass tanks filled with a clear fluid that each contained the body of an alien. The naked bodies had been stripped of their jumpsuits and now floated languidly in the preservative liquid.

The aliens were small humanoids, about three feet tall, with two arms and two legs. They had pale gray skin, bald heads, and large oblong eyes. They had two small vertical slits where one would expect to see a nose, and below was a slit that might have served as a mouth. There was no evidence of sex organs, so it was difficult to tell if they were male or female or asexual.

"Where is the other little alien?" I asked Albert.

"The third alien was completely dissected by a team of biologists to understand how its body functioned. They learned that the alien needed oxygen to breathe and its internal organs were similar to humans. They could not see any evidence of reproductive organs, and the biologists are still at a loss as to how these aliens reproduced. They did find what appeared to be a microchip implanted in its head, and they suspect it was used for communication with the mother ship.

"In reality, these little aliens are like worker bees in a hive. They were created by the advanced ETs from the mother ship through genetic engineering and creative mutations. They are the foot soldiers for this very advanced civilization who wanted expendable workers to conduct exploration activities in hostile environments. They do not have reproductive organs because they are cloned when new ones are needed. They are artificially created androids who serve a useful purpose for the ETs who created them."

"Do these little guys have souls?" I wondered, after trying to absorb all this information.

"No, they don't have souls, because they are more like mechanical robots than living creatures. The Council of Wise Ones that oversees the incarnations on their home planet decided they were not suitable vehicles for souls to occupy, and thus they are treated like computers and robots on Earth. They don't have feelings or emotions and don't have free will to take actions or make decisions, as they are programmed to follow orders without question and without any fear of what may happen to them as they carry out their missions. As a result of these factors, they were deemed not suitable for soul incarnations."

"What else can you show me about Area 51, Albert? I am keen to learn all I can."

Albert nodded his head as he led me out of this building toward another large structure nearby. I could hardly contain my excitement, as I anticipated another surprise.

Inside the third building there was a bustle of activity. On one side was a row of six little rooms, each with a large two-way mirror that allowed one to see into the rooms without being noticed. Outside of the rooms was a long bank of computer monitors and instrument panels, with people in white lab coats watching the screens intently.

When I peered into the rooms, I noticed each had one person sitting in a chair with an elaborate wire harness of cables fitted over the person's head. It was not apparent to me what was going on, so I looked to Albert for an explanation.

"What you are watching is a highly classified experiment to try to establish communications with souls on the Spirit Side," Albert explained. "The people in the rooms are psychics or mediums who volunteered for this project. Each of them has been successful in the past in speaking to, or receiving messages from, spirits from the Spirit Realm, and this project is designed to find out how they can pierce the veil to talk to spirits. They hope to be able to replicate these communication channels with powerful computers.

"So far, they have had no success. They can monitor the brain waves of the volunteers when they are communicating with the Other Side, and they have detected a distinct change to the brain waves when the communication is happening. But their supercomputers have not been able to contact spirits independently from the psychic/mediums.

"The reality is that the Council has blocked spirits from cooperating with this experiment because they fear it could be used for nefarious purposes. Imagine what a tool it would be for the military to be able to engage spirits to spy on military installations in other countries or to listen in on top-secret meetings of other governments. Not to mention how easy it would be for governments to invade the privacy of its citizens without being detected. It would lead to the ultimate Big Brother watching every move you make, something many world leaders would kill to achieve.

"And what is even worse, if they succeed in developing such a channel to the Spirit Side, they have plans to euthanize specially trained soldiers to do their bidding from the Spirit Realm as discarnate spies without the physical restrictions of a physical body.

"What they do not understand is that the soul of such a soldier, no matter how disciplined and duty-bound he or she may be, is not in any way obliged to follow the orders of the military brass after it leaves the physical body. Such souls would have a much different perspective of what is happening on Earth, and they would not do anything that could be invasive or harmful to anyone on your planet.

"Someday in your future, such communications may be allowed to a limited extent, but only for benevolent purposes. And right now, your civilization is not capable of using this technology for the benefit of all humans."

I nodded my concurrence with Albert and asked him if he had other things to show me in Area 51. Albert said there were many other interesting experiments and developments in this underground cavern, but they would have to wait. He had other things to show me, and I knew by now I should not question his agenda.

So, the mystery about Area 51 has been solved (at least partially), but it reminded me about some of the other mysteries of our world, and I decided to see what other information I could drag out of Albert.

# Chapter Twenty-Three
## Unveiling Secrets of the World

"I have a request for you, Albert. I have been dutifully following you on astral trips for several years. You get to choose where we go and who we talk to, and you never tell me why you take me on these excursions. I assume you have good reasons for the agenda you have planned for me, and I am OK with that. But I wonder if you would be willing to satisfy my curiosity about some of the unsolved mysteries I have come across during my life?"

"All right. I guess I owe you that much," Albert said somewhat reluctantly. "But keep in mind there are things I cannot reveal to you because the information might cause an unwanted disruption in human affairs on Earth. I will give you three topics to inquire about, and then we must resume my agenda."

"I understand, and I will not press you for information you feel would be inappropriate for general dissemination.

"My first question has to do with the Ark of the Covenant, which most scholars believe was the gold-covered wooden chest containing the original stone tablets inscribed with the Ten Commandments. I was fascinated by the movie *Raiders of the Lost Art* and have often wondered where the Ark currently resides and if it does have the supernatural powers depicted in the movie?"

"It does still exist," Albert responded. "Moses had the Ark of the Covenant built to hold the Ten Commandments, and the Israelites carried the Ark with them during the forty years they spent wandering in the desert. Eventually it was installed in the temple in Jerusalem. Several theories have been proposed about its current location, but a popular belief is that the Levitical priests moved the Ark to Egypt just before the Babylonians sacked Jerusalem in 586 BC, and it ended up in the town of Aksum, Ethiopia, in the cathedral of St. Mary of Zion. But because the church authorities will not permit anyone to examine this receptacle, its authenticity cannot be verified.

"The reality, however, is much different. Moses conceived the Ten Commandments after a period of deep meditation. He was searching for a set of rules he could present to his people as inspiration for a new way of living that would promote peace and prosperity among the Israelites. He knew his Commandments would have greater force if the people believed they were prescribed by a supreme being who could bestow good things on those people who followed his rules.

"For dramatic effect, Moses carved the commandments on two stone tablets but told his people they came from God. He also had the Ark built to hold the tablets, based on instructions he told them he had received from God.

"As you know from all our conversations, God (or the Source) does not manipulate events on Earth, and does not regard any actions of humans as right or wrong—they just are what they are as souls enjoy their journeys on the denser planes. The Ten Commandments did not come from the Source—they were engendered by Moses during his period of deep meditation.

"The Ark itself does not have any special properties or supernatural powers; it is merely a wooden chest that contains the stone tablets carved by Moses. It would be an archaeological treasure if it were found, but that is not likely to happen in the foreseeable future.

"The Ark was hidden by the Knights Templar at a secret location in France, where it remains today. Only two living people know its location, and they have sworn an oath to never disclose its hiding place. I am not going to tell you the exact location because that would endanger the Ark, but someday it will be put on display in a museum for all to see."

"Thanks for this information, Albert. My next question deals with the Bermuda Triangle (also known as the Devil's Triangle), which is a region in the western part of the North Atlantic Ocean where a number of aircraft and ships are said to have disappeared under mysterious circumstances. What can you tell me about this area?"

"The Bermuda Triangle is home to an ET base hidden under the seabed. The ETs use the base as a scouting outpost to monitor the activities of humans on Earth. Their spacecraft emit powerful electromagnetic waves that sometime interfere with the electronics in ships and airplanes, causing them to become disoriented and unable to communicate with land bases.

"The alien base also has a stargate or wormhole used to reach their home planet and other star systems. Sometimes ships and planes traversing the Triangle will get caught up in the energy vortex created by the wormhole, and they will quite literally disappear into a parallel universe."

"Why have we not discovered this ET base?" I wondered.

"The ETs, who are from a planet very distant from Earth, have very advanced technology, and they are able to easily conceal their underground base, as well as the comings and goings of their spaceships. Humans will not be able to detect the base until the ETs are ready to make open contact with all citizens of your planet. And as I mentioned before, at some point in the not-too-distant future all the ETs who have been monitoring Earth will openly reveal themselves when it is appropriate."

"My next question is with respect to the Loch Ness monster, a creature that has been sighted numerous times in Loch Ness. Does this fabled creature exist, and what type of animal is it?"

"This creature, known to most people as 'Nessie,' does exist in the deep waters of Loch Ness, Scotland. In fact, there is more than one Nessie in the lake, and they are the descendants of marine reptiles known as Elasmosaurus who lived in the late Cretaceous period. Most of these creatures perished with the dinosaurs around sixty-five million years ago, but a few survived. Several of them found their way into Loch Ness when it was still connected to the North Sea.

"They have a natural fear and distrust of humans, so they are careful to avoid detection, despite the efforts of all the human researchers. The deep waters of the Loch provide ample hiding places for them to conceal themselves, and they can communicate with each other over large distances under water using high-pitched chirps that function like sonar waves.

"They are harmless to humans, as they feed on the fish in the lake. So, the term 'monster' is a misnomer designed to draw tourists and curious researchers to the lake. My best advice to everyone is to leave them alone, so they can live their lives in peace without interference from humans."

"I get it, Albert. We both know that if one of these creatures was captured, it would be displayed in a zoo somewhere for people to gawk at and take photos. It is a pity humans like to house wild animals in cages, with little regard to the welfare of the animals. Although the zoo animals are well fed and cared for, there is no substitute for the ability to roam freely in their natural environments."

"This is true, my friend," Albert responded. "If you were able to communicate with the animals locked up in cages or compounds, they would all tell you their imprisonment is cruel treatment to creatures who were born to be free. In all cases, these animals, if given the choice, would choose death over a life in a cage, but they have no way of communicating this to the zookeepers who do not understand their plight.

"When you look into the eyes of a gorilla or tiger in captivity, you can detect a deep-seated melancholy spurred on by extreme boredom and frustration that they cannot do anything to change their circumstances. If they were able to take their own lives, they would do so in a flash."

"Have you ever incarnated as an animal on Earth?" I asked Albert.

"Yes, several times. In my last such incarnation, I was a female golden retriever living on a ranch in Wyoming. I was treated with kindness and respect by my owners, but things came off the rails when they decided I should have a litter of puppies. They arranged to borrow a stud from the neighbors and watched with amusement as he chased me around the yard. Eventually, he cornered me and consummated our nascent relationship. And he never even said thank you."

I chuckled at the pained expression on Albert's face, as I followed him back to planet Earth.

When I awoke the next morning in my physical body, I vividly remembered what I had experienced in my most recent astral trip, and I pounded out my notes on the keyboard as I sipped my morning coffee. Once finished, I thought about what I would ask Albert the next time he showed up in my bedroom, and the topic quickly popped up in mind: What else could he tell me about parallel universes?

As I waited for Albert to return, I recalled what I already knew about parallel universes.

# ⤖ Chapter Twenty-Four ⤖
## *Parallel Universes*

Many people through the ages have speculated that there is not only one universe but numerous parallel universes that exist simultaneously in different dimensions. Albert has confirmed to me that parallel universes do exist and have been around since the beginning of time.

When the Source created the first universe in what some scientists call the "Big Bang," it wanted to experience what it had created in all its facets without guidance or interference. So, the universe began as an explosion of pure energy that eventually congealed into matter in different patterns and formations. It was created with a built-in randomness factor to ensure the ongoing permutations would be limitless.

The first universe followed its divine destiny and eventually split into two universes, similar to the way a cell in a human body divides into two identical cells through the process known as mitosis. Although the two universes were identical at first, they soon began to develop on different paths due to the random interaction of their energy and matter. And then, at different times in the cosmic cycle, each of these two universes split into two, and so on until we now have countless universes all originally spawned from the Source.

No two universes are identical, although some have much in common while others are radically different. The differences arose initially due to small random variations in their flow of energy and the formation of matter, and later subtler distinctions resulted from the free will actions of the various life forms that populated the planets. In some universes, Earth does not even exist due to a quirk in the formation of the solar system. And in others, the planet is radically different from the world as we know it.

For example, in one parallel universe the asteroid that crashed into the Yucatan Peninsula sixty-five million years ago, killing most of the dinosaurs, missed that Earth by a whisker, and dinosaurs are still the dominant species of the planet. All these universes exist simultaneously in different dimensions, but most life forms, including humans on Earth, cannot detect them except in rare cases. There are, however, very advanced races that can peer into the other universes, and some can even travel between dimensions.

This brings to mind the so-called Mandela Effect, which has been discussed and debated for many years. The term was coined by a paranormal researcher who discovered that a significant number of participants at a conference in South Africa all had the same memory of media reports that Nelson Mandela had died in prison in the 1980s, in stark contrast with the fact he had been released from prison in 1990 and went on to become president of that country. Several explanations have been advanced for this phenomenon, but the reality, according to Albert, is these people had a glimpse of Earth in a parallel universe where the events they remember about Mandela were actually true.

Albert explained that sometimes windows to other dimensions will temporarily open up, allowing people to view the events in another dimension that often have significant differences from our own dimension.

To make his point, Albert took me on an astral trip to visit Earth in another dimension. He led me through an interdimensional doorway floating in space high above our planet. On the other side, we hovered momentarily above a blue orb that looked like Earth, before we plunged down through the clouds on our way to New York City. When we landed in lower Manhattan, I was surprised to see the World Trade towers standing intact, as I remembered them from one of my visits to the city prior to September 11, 2001. Albert explained it was the same year in this universe as in our world, and the World Trade towers were still standing because they had not been destroyed in a terrorist attack in 2001 due to the fact there were no Islamic terrorists in this world.

In fact, Islam as a religion did not exist anywhere on this planet, because Muhammad died at a young age before he was able to engender the religion that currently plays a major role in world affairs on our Earth. As a result, the Middle Eastern countries on this planet were mostly Christian, and there were no jihadists anywhere.

He pointed out a number of significant differences that arose from this one seminal event. The Crusades did not happen, because the Holy Land was occupied by Christians, not infidels. The state of Israel did not exist, and the territory occupied by Israel, Lebanon, Syria, and the Sinai Peninsula in our world comprise the country of Palestine in this world, which is populated by Jews and Christian Arabs who live in peaceful coexistence. There was no civil war in the lands comprising our Syria, and ISIS never existed.

And then to demonstrate another significant difference, Albert took me north to the heart of Harlem. When I asked him why there were so few African Americans on the streets, he said it resulted from another noteworthy event on this planet that never happened on our Earth. Early in the sixteenth century, England abolished slavery and the rest of Europe soon followed suit. And because the colonies in North America were governed by England and other European nations, slavery was also abolished in the New World.

This meant no slaves were captured in Africa and transported to America, and African Americans, who immigrated to America in the normal course, represented less than 1 percent of the population of the United States (rather than the 13 percent in our world), and they were scattered over the whole country. President Lincoln did not issue the Emancipation Proclamation because there were no slaves to free, and the Civil War never happened. There was no need for the civil rights movement, and there was no such thing as the Confederate flag or the Ku Klux Klan.

I was truly astounded at how a couple of seemingly minor quirks in the history of that Earth had such a major effect in the development of the planet.

This was one example of our planet in a parallel universe, and one can only imagine what one would find in all the other universes that have planets similar to Earth. So, what happens to the inhabitants of Earth when our universe splits into two? Albert says everything in the universe, including the life forms, split into two parts that are initially identical. But as the linear time of the denser planes marches on, subtle changes begin to appear, often resulting in significant differences between the two universes.

Thus, it is possible an individual human on our planet has one or more "clones" living in one or more parallel Earths where their circumstances could be very dissimilar. Because we all make free will choices, a person's "cosmic twin" may have a different spouse, children, or job and may live in a different city or country than the person in our Earth. It would be fascinating, indeed, if we were able to view ourselves in these parallel dimensions to see how our free will decisions turned out compared with the outcomes enjoyed by our cosmic twins.

Most of us have looked back on our lives and wondered how things would have unfolded if we had made a different choice at various decision points in our history. What if we had chosen a different job, missed the party where we met our spouse and ended up marrying someone else, or decided to live in a different part of the country? While the result would no doubt be different, would we have ended up in a better or worse position? If we could only peer into the other dimension, we would know the result.

Perhaps it is best we are not allowed to know the details of our parallel lives, because it could be distracting or even burdensome to have such knowledge, as we might spend too much of our time kicking ourselves for making bad decisions or gloating about how smart we were compared to our cosmic clones.

There are no absolute right or wrong decisions or paths to follow during our incarnations. Every life has its own lessons and challenges, and it is not possible to say one life was better than another. A life filled with success and wealth is not inherently better than a life of squalor. What is important is how we deal with the events that unfold after we make our free will choices, and this is what determines the extent to which a life has helped us grow and evolve as souls. Our goal is to learn everything we can from our incarnations on Earth in all its dimensions so we can graduate from this school and move on to other adventures.

When Albert next appeared in my life, I was ready with my questions about parallel universes.

# ~Chapter Twenty-Five ~
## *Cosmic Twins*

"A question for you, Albert, about parallel dimensions. In how many of them does planet Earth exist?"

"There are numerous parallel dimensions with Earth in them, far too many to count," Albert responded.

I continued: "You mentioned previously that the parallel universes result from the division of one universe into two universes, a process that has been happening since the first universe was created long ago. What happens if I am living in a universe when it splits into two?"

"In such case," Albert explained, "your human body would also be split into two identical bodies, each living in its own universe. You would not be aware this had happened, as there would be no noticeable changes to you or your planet. Eventually, as time marches on, the two Garnets would begin to differ due the random interaction of energy and matter in each of the universes.

"Some of the differences would result from physical

changes in the universes, while other distinctions would result from the decisions and actions of the two Garnets and the other humans on the planets. For example, as time progresses from the splitting of the original universe, actions and decisions made by various world governments could affect Garnet differently in each universe. Elections, revolts, wars, and other macro changes in the world affairs could influence the two Garnets in different ways, and their respective paths could end up being much different.

"As well, the individual decisions and actions taken by the two humans could also send them on markedly different paths. If you look back on your life, you will recall you faced many different decision points in your life, where you had to choose one path over another. This includes things like choosing your career path, picking your spouse, choosing a city to live in, and deciding which offer of employment to accept.

"As you recall, most of these decisions were difficult to make, because the alternatives were often equally attractive. It would not be hard to imagine you and your clone could have chosen different paths when you came to these forks in the road. And such crucial decisions could have major consequences as time progressed. When you look back at these major inflection points, you may wonder what would have happened if you had made a different choice. While you cannot go back in time to change these decisions, it is possible one of your clones in a parallel universe did choose the other path. The result of such decision would be available for you to see in the Akashic Records after you transition to the Spirit Side."

"That would be fascinating, indeed, Albert. Is there any way I can view these parallel lives right now?"

"You are not permitted to view these lives during your time on Earth because it could be too disruptive to your journey. If you saw the life of one of your clones that turned out better, in your opinion, than your current life, you would spend too much time agonizing over why you didn't make the same decisions as your clone. And harshly judging your actions with the benefit of this 'hindsight' would serve no useful purpose."

"What happens to my soul when the universe divides and there is now two of me?" I queried Albert.

"Most often, your soul would continue to dwell in both Garnets, as it is possible for a soul to be in more than one physical entity at the same time. When both of you die and transition to the Spirit Side, both facets of your soul will be reunited. Instead of one life to review in your Life Review, you would have two lives to review and the differences in the outcomes of those two lives would provide your soul with an even greater understanding of how your actions affected your ability to overcome the challenges and learn the lessons you had hoped to achieve.

"Keep in mind there is no 'right' or 'wrong' path for anyone to follow. From your perspective as a human, you might think one of your clones had a better life than the other, because one was more successful in his career or was able to accumulate more wealth, but such criteria are not important on the Spirit Side. Every journey on the denser planes has value for the soul regardless of whether or not it was successful from a human perspective."

"I take it you are not going to show me a parallel universe where one of my clones exists."

"That is right, for the reasons I have stated. Sometime in the future, I may take you to other parallel universes where you do not have a clone. This is the best I can do, so you will have to live with it."

"As usual, Albert, I know it is fruitless to argue with you. I await our next adventure with bated breath."

After reflecting on what I had learned about parallel universes, I pressed Albert for a chance to visit another parallel Earth, and so off we went to continue my exploration of the universe. Albert was close-lipped about our next destination, but I knew I would not be disappointed.

# Chapter Twenty-Six
## *Beam Me Up*

Once again Albert led me through the interdimensional doorway to Earth in a parallel universe. From space, it looked like our Earth, but I soon noticed some differences as we descended to the surface.

As we approached Los Angeles on the west coast of America, I noticed the air above the city was crystal clear, without the smog that usually blankets the city. The freeways and streets below were all devoid of vehicles, with only a few people walking, jogging, or rollerblading in the bright sunlight. I wondered what catastrophe had transformed this once bustling city into a virtual ghost town.

Albert sensed my confusion, and he explained: "This Earth is in the same time frame as your Earth, but it has progressed on a much different path than your world. Early in the twenty-first century, this planet also had a coronavirus pandemic, and the lockdowns continued for several months until a group of scientists in China discovered a drug that successfully treated the infection in people. Soon thereafter, a vaccine was developed and distributed widely around the globe, and this put an end to the pandemic.

"The people of this world noticed during the lockdown that the air, rivers, and lakes all over the world had become less polluted due to the great decrease in vehicular traffic, industrial production, and social interaction. And they liked what they saw. So, when the crisis had subsided, many countries decided it was a top priority to find a way to allow people to enjoy a happy and healthy way of life without polluting Mother Earth. They realized the biggest obstacle to achieving this goal was the need for people and goods to move freely around the cities and between cities and countries. They understood this movement of people and goods was the cause of most of the pollution generated by humans, because the transportation system, for the most part, burned fossil fuels.

"As a result, billions of dollars were funneled to research projects to find a way to transport people and freight without any pollution. To make a long story short, a few years after the Covid-19 pandemic scientists at the European Organization for Nuclear Research in Geneva, commonly known as CERN, found a way to dematerialize a water molecule and rematerialize it at another location, without any changes to its molecular structure.

"This breakthrough caused a flurry of activity around

the world as scientists from other countries were able to replicate this phenomenon, as they searched for practical applications for this amazing discovery. Eventually, through trial and error, they found a way to dematerialize virtually any matter, including living creatures, and rematerialize it thousands of miles away without any changes to the objects that were transported.

"They eventually developed machines, not unlike the teleportation machines in *Star Trek*, that were deployed throughout the world to transport people and freight without the need for fossil-fuel-burning vehicles. This is why streets and freeways in their cities are not jammed with cars and trucks—as all freight and people are moved around the city, the country, and the world with these transporters. You see, Gene Roddenberry, who created *Star Trek*, had the right idea, but the science on your Earth has not yet achieved the breakthrough this Earth did so successfully.

"And you can well imagine the astounding difference these machines made on their society. People did not need vehicles to travel around the city to go to work or school or to shop for food and clothing, nor did they need to go to airports to catch a plane to another city.

"In your Earth, if you want to visit another city, you have to book a flight, take a car or taxi to the airport, stand in line to check in, stand in another line to go through security, que up to get on the plane, and then sit in cramped seating for several hours until you land at your destination. On this Earth, all you must do is go to one of the teleportation stations near you (and they have one every few blocks), dial in your destination, and press 'Go.' In the blink of an eye, you will find yourself in a station in your destination city, none the worse for the wear. It's like magic!

"Although man-made pollution has not been eradicated entirely, it has been drastically reduced due to the dearth of vehicles (including cars, trucks, trains, and airplanes) belching noxious fumes into the atmosphere. This is why there is no smog in this city or anywhere else on this planet, and the rivers and lakes are so crystal clear.

"Their space program was totally upended by these teleporters, as they could now transport people and materials to the Moon, Mars, and other planets and moons in the solar system without the need for booster rockets. In fact, this civilization has domed colonies on several of their celestial neighbors orbiting their sun, and humans and equipment can now travel between these outposts with relative ease."

"I am flabbergasted, Albert, at the difference the teleporter has made to this civilization and their planet. Can you please tell me (and the scientists back on my Earth) the secret to making these teleportation devices, so my Earth can achieve the same transformation?"

"Alas, as much as I would like to help the people on your planet, I cannot give you the information you need because I would run afoul of the prime directive. Souls on the Spirit Side adhere to the same principles as the members of the Galactic Federation, which prohibit us from unduly interfering with the development of civilizations in our galaxy. We cannot give you the blueprint for these machines on a silver platter; you must discover the formula on your own through hard work and determination. But we can offer subtle assistance by sending intuitive messages to your scientists, and it is up to them to take the next steps."

"I was afraid you were going to say that, Albert, but I thought I should ask the question anyway. Do you foresee these devices being developed in the future for my planet?"

Albert paused for a moment, and then continued: "There is no doubt such teleporter devices will someday become an important part of the civilization on your Earth, provided you don't destroy yourselves or your planet before that day arrives. There are no guarantees, but I am confident humanity on Earth will survive to enjoy the benefits of advanced technology like the people on this planet."

On that note, Albert motioned for me to follow him

up through the clouds as we headed back to my Earth where I could once again partake in the joys of traveling in a vehicle stuck in traffic or being squished into a tiny seat on a flying tube with wings.

When Albert appeared in my bedroom once again in the dead of the night, I wondered what he had up his sleeve this time.

# Chapter Twenty-Seven
## Three Wise Men

"Where are we going tonight?" I asked Albert.

"Back to the Spirit Side. I want you to listen in on a conversation you will find very interesting," Albert responded with a sly grin.

So off we went. Albert took me into the Hall of Wisdom where I noticed three souls sitting in front of the Council of Wise Ones—Jesus, Moses, and Muhammad. I settled down on a bench to one side of the large chamber and listened with intense interest.

Sophia, the Chair of the Council, spoke to the three wise men: "Welcome, dear souls, and thank you for joining us today. The Council has been discussing a matter of grave concern for planet Earth, and we wanted to get your input.

"The three of you have had a huge influence on the development of human civilization since you walked the Earth, and we seek your sage advice on where we go from here. As you know, humans have been struggling to attain enlightenment ever since they first appeared on Earth, and we fear they may not survive without strong intervention from this side of the veil.

"There are too many people who let their toxic emotions rule their actions and not enough people who embrace love and compassion. This results in violence and abuse to their fellow humans, to Mother Earth, and to the other creatures who live on the planet. This must be stopped before they destroy their civilization and render the planet barren of all life.

"The Council believes the best way to salvage the mess on the planet is to send them a new messiah— someone who will lead them out of the cesspool of darkness and into a new era of enlightenment. We welcome your thoughts on our proposal."

Jesus spoke first: "I assume you intend one of us to incarnate again as a human. Does the incarnation have to begin at the birth of a baby, or could we enter a more mature body as a walk-in?"

"Given the urgency of the matter, it would be quicker for you to go as a walk-in soul. This way you can begin your mission immediately without having to wait for your body to mature into an adult," Sophia responded. "We have not yet picked a suitable life for you to take over, but we will work with the chosen candidate to find a person and country that would give you the best platform for your mission."

"Will the chosen one be able to utilize the power of focused thoughts to perform 'miracles'?" Muhammad asked.

"Yes," Sophia replied. "In order to have the most impact and attract attention, you would be able to use such powers. You will have to be very judicious in using this capability, because it could distract from your message. People might be too focused on the 'miracles' to fully absorb your teachings. It would not be useful to the cause if you ended up being viewed as a circus side show."

"Do you expect the candidate would start a new religion?" Moses wondered.

"We don't think a new religion is the answer," Sophia explained. "As you know, the religions currently existing on Earth have not solved the problems, and in many cases, religions have exacerbated the violence among humans. The Crusades and the Inquisitions are examples of torture and killings encouraged by Christian holy men, and most of the recent terrorist acts by Islamic Jihadists have used their religion as a justification for their actions.

"Religions have done plenty of good deeds in the past, but they are too susceptible to being hijacked by their leaders who use them as a way to control the masses to further their own agendas, which are often not designed to foster love and peace among humans.

"We think the best approach for the candidate is to engender a movement to encourage people to attain spiritual enlightenment without the hierarchy and structure of an organized religion. We have not settled on how this should be done, and we welcome your input."

"Do you think the human chosen for this incarnation should be male or female?" Jesus asked.

"It depends on where the person lives," Sophia responded. "In some extreme patriarchal countries women are not regarded as equal to men, and it would be difficult for a female to lead the kind of spiritual movement we contemplate. Even in more progressive societies, women may not be accepted in leadership roles as much as men. We certainly think a woman should be given a chance to fill this role, but we question whether the world is ready for a female messiah."

"You are right to have misgivings about this," Muhammad noted. "There are many Islamic countries where a woman would have little chance of leading such a movement, I am embarrassed to acknowledge. Although I founded this religion, I did not intend it to be used to justify the subjugation and abuse of women. I had hoped women would be treated as equals, but that remains an elusive goal in many Muslim countries."

Moses seemed to be in deep contemplation, and then he verbalized his thoughts: "Maybe that is what humanity needs to gain spiritual traction. If a female messiah can reform these harsh patriarchal societies, the rest of the world would easily fall into place. If the movement starts in the Western world, Muslims may regard it with suspicion. They might dismiss it as another example of Western decadence."

"I get your meaning, Moses," Jesus responded. "But if the movement originates in a Muslim country, a female messiah might be beaten or killed before she could fully develop her mission. I think it would be easier for a woman to gain prominence in an egalitarian society, and then use it as a springboard to reform the other countries."

"These are all good points to consider, gentlemen," Sophia jumped in. "There seems to be a consensus that a female messiah would find it more difficult to carry out the task we contemplate, but not impossible. I think it best the chosen candidate should be free to choose the human they will use to carry out this mission, whether it be as a male or female.

"And now the big question. Which of you three will volunteer for this assignment?"

Without hesitation, all three wise men raised their hands.

"Fantastic," Sophia exclaimed. "Come with me to the Hall of Planning and together we will find a suitable candidate for you to walk into when the time is right.

And since you are all eager to do your part, we will also consider having all three of you incarnate at the same time. One could be the messiah, and the other two could be his or her trusted lieutenants."

Jesus, Muhammad, and Moses nodded in agreement, as they followed Sophia out of the chamber. I was keen to follow this esteemed group to see what transpired, but Albert held me back.

"I am sorry, but you are not allowed to learn about the details of this mission, because it must be kept quiet until it has been launched. Suffice it to say it will happen in some form, although the timing must remain a secret," Albert confirmed.

"How will I know who is the chosen one?" I wondered.

"You will know it when you see it. And if it doesn't happen until after you transition to the Spirit Side, you can watch all the action from there," Albert replied.

I knew there was no point in pressing Albert for more information, but I was elated to know help was on the way. Maybe there was hope for my planet after all.

Albert and I strolled down the main boulevard of Aglaia amid the throngs of souls who went about their business with a joyfulness that warmed my heart. As we sat down on a bench on one corner of the main plaza, I could see something was on Albert's mind, so I waited patiently for him to speak.

# ∾Chapter Twenty-Eight ∾
## *Adieu*

"The time has come for me to bid you farewell for the time being," Albert announced. "I have been recruited by Sophia to work with the three wise men to develop a Life Plan for the new messiah. As one of your spirit guides, I will always be there for you, but I will put our astral trips on hold for awhile and let your other guides take charge until I return.

"I trust you enjoyed our adventures on the astral plane and hope you learned a few things to help you with the dance of life on Earth. Over here, you can dance with the angels in a joyful, carefree frolic. But on Earth, you must choose between a dance of joy or a dance of despair, and which one you choose will dictate how happy or sorrowful your journey will be. Be sure to choose wisely.

"Always remember you are on an adventure you chose for yourself. Do not take life too seriously because, as a wise man once said, you will never come out of it alive. Strive to enjoy all your experiences as a soul having a human journey, because you can never go wrong or become lost, no matter how many times you stray off course. Smile at everyone you meet, laugh often, and relish your role as an individual aspect of the Source. And above all, fill your heart with love and compassion for yourself, all other humans, the creatures who share your planet, and Mother Earth herself.

"As a practical matter, I encourage you to write the manuscript for your fifth book before you lose all your faculties. It would be next to impossible to write a book if you spend most of your day sitting slack-jawed on a park bench feeding the pigeons."

"Thanks a lot, Albert, for your vote of confidence. Do me a favor, though. If I ever get to that stage, please give me directions on where to find the 'stairway to heaven' so I can cast aside the surly bonds of Earth and soar with the eagles."

"Consider it done," Albert said with a wink, as he escorted me back to my bedroom.

When I rose the next morning, I had a sinking feeling there would be a large gap in my life without Albert. I could only hope I would see him again soon. Until then, life must go on …

# Praise for Dancing with Angels in Heaven

Garnet Schulhauser's *Dancing with Angels in Heaven* is another great work of his. The book is challenging to put down. The author's journey with Albert, his spirit guide, to Aglaia answers many of the eternal questions that we all have. Topics such as developing a soul's life plan prior to incarnating, why incarnate, meeting with the Council of Wise Ones to prepare for life on earth, what souls chose to experience in the afterlife, parallel universes, the pandemic and more. This book is absolutely fascinating and brilliantly written. Get ready to transverse the universe with Albert and Garnet Schulhauser, it's an astounding experience.

**Valerie Camozzi, RN, and Quantum Healing Hypnosis Technique Practitioner**

Garnet Schulhauser's fifth book, *Dancing with Angels in Heaven*, is a delightful read which will not only have you chuckling at the ongoing comic stick between Garnet and his Angel Guide Albert, but will leave you feeling comforted.

On this adventure with Albert, Garnet learns the intricacies of the soul's journey from creation to incarnation and back to "heaven". Many of those hard questions we all ponder are discussed. I was left with a feeling of peace, that we are here on purpose and that we return to bliss when our time on earth is done.

**Rhonda Elliott, Reiki Master/Teacher and co-host of Spirit Sessions, a View of the light**

Dancing with Angels in Heaven is the crown jewel of one my favorite spiritual book series of all time and I highly recommend it. Garnet and Albert are back to lead us on more fascinating adventures to the spirit side so we might peak behind the curtains once more. As to be expected, we are introduced to a variety of characters, some old and some new, that have a brilliant and sometimes comical way of relaying fascinating spiritual insights. Most importantly, this book has a very serious and time sensitive message with instructions for the next steps humanity must take for our growth and evolution.

**Jonny Enoch, Host of Mystery Teachings on Gaia**

Congratulations, Garnet, for writing yet another book chock-full of mind-boggling information that caused a feeling of peace, harmony and hope to well up within me. This book brings it all together completely and expertly.

Thank you, Garnet, for writing your five books providing the reader step-by-step insights along the way and important, thought-provoking information.

I suggest that you purchase all of Garnet's books and see for yourself what reading and studying does for you. I have had the privilege of interviewing Garnet Schulhauser as a guest on my monthly radio talk show several times, and he was very well received by my listening audience.

**Dr. Anne Marie Evers, Author & Counsellor**

Prepare to be entertained, humoured, moved, and challenged to evolve! It is rare to find a fellow lawyer, an adept of the material world, so eloquently relaying the often bizarre, profound, and thought-provoking experiences from the spiritual realm made possible through the astral body.

This is a book of hope for Mankind, faith in the Divine and describes a logic of the Soul. The latest messages are neatly bound together with signature threads of direct reporting, careful clarity and cool pragmatism in the face of significant and often unusual encounters that expose the boundaries of what we think is possible contrasted to "what is" or "may be" the case.

Ultimately, the following pages gently comfort and invite you, the reader, to self-question, interpretate and work on your life all the while making a better world and embracing the journey of infinite consciousness towards the Light. Bon voyage!

**J.P. Hague, lawyer, researcher & writer**

Many years ago, Garnet Schulhauser left his lucrative law practice after someone incredibly wise and immensely kind challenged him to consider a far richer way to live. In the process, one that asked much of the author but returned vastly more, Garnet dug deep into his soul to discover "the ineffable joy of spiritual enlightenment." He has not stopped writing and talking about it since. So, it is with bringers of glad tidings: they invite us to join in the cosmic dance and work it until we realize that the music never ends.

**Gary Mantz and Suzanne Mitchell, hosts of The Mantz and Mitchell Show on 1150 KKNW Seattle**

# *About the Author*

## Garnet Schulhauser

Garnet Schulhauser is a lawyer who practiced corporate law for over thirty years with two blue-chip law firms in Calgary until he retired in 2008. Since then, he has published five books in the spiritual/metaphysical genre: *Dancing on a Stamp, Dancing Forever with Spirit, Dance of Heavenly Bliss, Dance of Eternal Rapture,* and *Dancing with Angels in Heaven,* which recount his dialogue and astral travels with his spirit guide, Albert, who confronted him on the street one day disguised as a homeless man. His books answer the eternal questions of life, as he reveals the truth about our existence as eternal souls, the cycle of reincarnation and the role of karma, the splendor of the afterlife that awaits us all, and the diversity of life in our vast universe.

Since the release of his first book, Garnet has been active with book signing tours and conference presentations and has been interviewed on over one hundred sixty radio talk shows broadcast from studios around the world. In addition, Garnet is a Level 2 Quantum Healing Hypnosis Technique (QHHT) Practitioner, a modality that guides clients to experience past lives and connect with their Higher Selves.

For more information about Garnet, his books, and QHHT, please visit his websites:

www.garnetschulhauser.com

www.garnetschulhauserqhht.com

# Books by Garnet Schulhauser

**Dancing on a Stamp**
Published by: Ozark Mountain Publishing

**Dancing Forever with Spirit**
Published by: Ozark Mountain Publishing

**Dance of Heavenly Bliss**
Published by: Ozark Mountain Publishing

**Dance of Eternal Rapture**
Published by: Ozark Mountain Publishing

**Dancing with Angels in Heaven**
Published by: Ozark Mountain Publishing

For more information about any of the above titles, soon to be released titles,
or other items in our catalog, write, phone or visit our website:
Ozark Mountain Publishing, Inc.
PO Box 754, Huntsville, AR 72740
479-738-2348/800-935-0045
www.ozarkmt.com

# If you liked this book, you might also like:

*Application of Impossible Things*
by Natalie Sudman
*Avoiding Karma*
by Guy Needler
*Baby It's You*
by Maureen McGill
*Croton*
by Artur Tadevosyan
*In Light and In Shade*
by Patricia Irvine
*Judy's Story*
by L.R. Sumpter
*Ghost and Me*
by Kevin Killen
*Not Your Average Angel Book*
By Andy Myers
*The Anne Dialogues*
By Guy Needler

For more information about any of the above titles, soon to be released titles,
or other items in our catalog, write, phone or visit our website:
Ozark Mountain Publishing, LLC
PO Box 754, Huntsville, AR 72740
479-738-2348
www.ozarkmt.com

OZARK
MOUNTAIN
PUBLISHING

For more information about any of the titles published by Ozark Mountain Publishing, Inc., soon to be released titles, or other items in our catalog, write, phone or visit our website:

Ozark Mountain Publishing, Inc.

PO Box 754

Huntsville, AR 72740


479-738-2348/800-935-0045

www.ozarkmt.com

# Other Books by Ozark Mountain Publishing, Inc.

**Dolores Cannon**
A Soul Remembers Hiroshima
Between Death and Life
Conversations with Nostradamus,
   Volume I, II, III
The Convoluted Universe -Book One,
   Two, Three, Four, Five
The Custodians
Five Lives Remembered
Jesus and the Essenes
Keepers of the Garden
Legacy from the Stars
The Legend of Starcrash
The Search for Hidden Sacred
Knowledge
They Walked with Jesus
The Three Waves of Volunteers and the
   New Earth
**Aron Abrahamsen**
Holiday in Heaven
Out of the Archives – Earth Changes
**James Ream Adams**
Little Steps
**Justine Alessi & M. E. McMillan**
Rebirth of the Oracle
**Kathryn/Patrick Andries**
Naked in Public
**Kathryn Andries**
The Big Desire
Dream Doctor
Soul Choices: Six Paths to Find Your
   Life Purpose
Soul Choices: Six Paths to Fulfilling
   Relationships
**Patrick Andries**
Owners Manual for the Mind
**Cat Baldwin**
Divine Gifts of Healing
**Dan Bird**
Finding Your Way in the Spiritual Age
Waking Up in the Spiritual Age
**Julia Cannon**
Soul Speak – The Language of Your
Body
**Ronald Chapman**
Seeing True
**Albert Cheung**
The Emperor's Stargate
**Jack Churchward**
Lifting the Veil on the Lost Continent of
   Mu
The Stone Tablets of Mu
**Sherri Cortland**
Guide Group Fridays

Raising Our Vibrations for the New
   Age
Spiritual Tool Box
Windows of Opportunity
**Patrick De Haan**
The Alien Handbook
**Paulinne Delcour-Min**
Spiritual Gold
Holly Ice
Divine Fire
**Joanne DiMaggio**
Edgar Cayce and the Unfulfilled
   Destiny of Thomas Jefferson
   Reborn
**Anthony DeNino**
The Power of Giving and Gratitude
**Michael Dennis**
Morning Coffee with God
God's Many Mansions
**Carolyn Greer Daly**
Opening to Fullness of Spirit
**Anita Holmes**
Twidders
**Aaron Hoopes**
Reconnecting to the Earth
**Victoria Hunt**
Kiss the Wind
**Patricia Irvine**
In Light and In Shade
**Kevin Killen**
Ghosts and Me
**Diane Lewis**
From Psychic to Soul
**Donna Lynn**
From Fear to Love
**Maureen McGill**
Baby It's You
**Maureen McGill & Nola Davis**
Live from the Other Side
**Curt Melliger**
Heaven Here on Earth
Where the Weeds Grow
**Henry Michaelson**
And Jesus Said – A Conversation
**Dennis Milner**
Kosmos
**Andy Myers**
Not Your Average Angel Book
**Guy Needler**
Avoiding Karma
Beyond the Source – Book 1, Book 2
The History of God
The Origin Speaks

For more information about any of the above titles, soon to be released titles,
or other items in our catalog, write, phone or visit our website:
PO Box 754, Huntsville, AR 72740
479-738-2348/800-935-0045
www.ozarkmt.com

# Other Books by Ozark Mountain Publishing, Inc.

The Anne Dialogues
The Curators
Psycho Spiritual Healing
**James Nussbaumer**
And Then I Knew My Abundance
The Master of Everything
Mastering Your Own Spiritual Freedom
Living Your Dram, Not Someone Else's
**Sherry O'Brian**
Peaks and Valleys
**Riet Okken**
The Liberating Power of Emotions
**Gabrielle Orr**
Akashic Records: One True Love
Let Miracles Happen
**Victor Parachin**
Sit a Bit
**Nikki Pattillo**
A Spiritual Evolution
Children of the Stars
**Rev. Grant H. Pealer**
A Funny Thing Happened on the
    Way to Heaven
Worlds Beyond Death
**Victoria Pendragon**
Born Healers
Feng Shui from the Inside, Out
Sleep Magic
The Sleeping Phoenix
Being In A Body
**Michael Perlin**
Fantastic Adventures in Metaphysics
**Walter Pullen**
Evolution of the Spirit
**Debra Rayburn**
Let's Get Natural with Herbs
**Charmian Redwood**
A New Earth Rising
Coming Home to Lemuria
**David Rivinus**
Always Dreaming
**Richard Rowe**
Imagining the Unimaginable
Exploring the Divine Library
**M. Don Schorn**
Elder Gods of Antiquity
Legacy of the Elder Gods
Gardens of the Elder Gods
Reincarnation...Stepping Stones of Life
**Garnet Schulhauser**
Dancing on a Stamp
Dancing Forever with Spirit

Dance of Heavenly Bliss
Dance of Eternal Rapture
Dancing with Angels in Heaven
**Manuella Stoerzer**
Headless Chicken
**Annie Stillwater Gray**
Education of a Guardian Angel
The Dawn Book
Work of a Guardian Angel
Joys of a Guardian Angel
**Blair Styra**
Don't Change the Channel
Who Catharted
**Natalie Sudman**
Application of Impossible Things
**L.R. Sumpter**
Judy's Story
The Old is New
We Are the Creators
**Artur Tradevosyan**
Croton
**Jim Thomas**
Tales from the Trance
**Jolene and Jason Tierney**
A Quest of Transcendence
**Paul Travers**
Dancing with the Mountains
**Nicholas Vesey**
Living the Life-Force
**Janie Wells**
Embracing the Human Journey
Payment for Passage
**Dennis Wheatley/ Maria Wheatley**
The Essential Dowsing Guide
**Maria Wheatley**
Druidic Soul Star Astrology
**Jacquelyn Wiersma**
The Zodiac Recipe
**Sherry Wilde**
The Forgotten Promise
**Lyn Willmott**
A Small Book of Comfort
Beyond all Boundaries Book 1
**Stuart Wilson & Joanna Prentis**
Atlantis and the New Consciousness
Beyond Limitations
The Essenes -Children of the Light
The Magdalene Version
Power of the Magdalene
**Robert Winterhalter**
The Healing Christ

For more information about any of the above titles, soon to be released titles,
or other items in our catalog, write, phone or visit our website:
PO Box 754, Huntsville, AR 72740
479-738-2348/800-935-0045
www.ozarkmt.com